Horses
Never Lie

2nd Edition

Also by Mark Rashid

A Good Horse Is Never a Bad Color
with Illustrations by Herb Mignery

Considering the Horse:
Tales of Problems Solved and Lessons Learned
with Illustrations by Ron Ball

Whole Heart, Whole Horse:
Building Trust Between Horse and Rider

Horses Never Lie

2nd Edition

The Heart of Passive Leadership

Mark Rashid
Foreword by Rick Lamb

Skyhorse Publishing

Skyhorse Publishing books may be purchased in bulk at special discounts for sales promotion, corporate gifts, fund-raising, or educational purposes. Special editions can also be created to specifications. For details, contact the Special Sales Department, Skyhorse Publishing, 307 West 36th Street, 11th Floor, New York, NY 10018 or info@skyhorsepublishing.com.

Skyhorse® and Skyhorse Publishing® are registered trademarks of Skyhorse Publishing, Inc.®, a Delaware corporation.

Visit our website at www.skyhorsepublishing.com.

15 14 13 12

Library of Congress Cataloging-in-Publication Data is available on file.

Cover design by Liz Driesbach

Print ISBN: 978-1-63450-255-9
Ebook ISBN: 978-1-62873-004-3

Printed in the United States of America

For all the people around the world that have allowed me the great honor of working with them and their horses.

Contents

Foreword

My first exposure to Mark Rashid cost me a good night's sleep. It was a Thursday evening in late 1997 and I was to record a radio interview with him the following morning on his first book, *Considering the Horse*. I figured an hour or so would be enough to get up to speed on his training methods and to scribble out a few insightful questions on my beat-up yellow pad. So I settled at my desk, opened the book, and launched into skimming mode. Now, I've gotten pretty good at skimming, and most horse-training books lend themselves to that since they're written like textbooks. This book was different, however, and before I realized it, I was hooked. I read into the wee hours of Friday morning and forgot all about my yellow pad.

I read every word of that book, then later, its sequel, *A Good Horse is Never a Bad Color*, as well as the book you now hold in your hands, which Mark was kind enough to send me, chapter-by-recently-completed-chapter, via e-mail. I'll admit it: I'm a fan.

Mark Rashid is a unique and thoughtful horse trainer whose insistence on considering the horse's point of view is producing remarkable changes in horses and the people who love them. He's also a fine storyteller who manages to weave the horsemanship principles he espouses seamlessly into engaging anecdotes taken from his own life, especially his boyhood tutelage under a grizzled old horseman he refers to simply as *the old man*. I suspect that you will find yourself, as I have, reliving in Mark's stories your own youth, a time that could be bittersweet, confusing, and exhilarating, all on the same day.

Mark Rashid bases his gentle, non-assertive horse-training philosophy on the *passive leader*, the horse in the herd who leads by example rather than force. I've noticed that this is a good description of the man himself. Mark will not force his methods down your throat any more than he would force them on a horse. He'll simply lay out the choices as he sees them and let you decide for yourself.

Take it from an expert. This is not a book for skimming. You'll want to keep it on your nightstand, savor every word, and dream sweet, horsey dreams. Who knows? You may wake up a better horseman, and a better person.

—*Rick Lamb*

The Horse Show, syndicated radio program

Introduction: What is a Passive Leader?

Back in the spring of 1996, I was asked to give a lecture for the Pacific Northwest Endurance Riders' Convention that was to be held in Oregon. The subject matter for the lecture was left up to me, but the organizer mentioned that she felt a lot of the folks who were going to attend might be interested in hearing about how I work with troubled horses.

I gave the idea a great deal of thought before finally sitting down at the computer and trying to jot down some notes. For some reason, I was having a very difficult time getting my thoughts together for the speech, and it took me nearly six months to get an outline down on paper. Even at that, I still wasn't overly excited about what I had written. I had given so many talks on troubled horses over the years that I couldn't help but feel like I would be repeating myself by giving this talk. Even so, it was what they wanted to hear, so I figured I would go on ahead and give the talk as I had outlined it.

I was to give the speech around mid-February of 1997 and had only finished my notes on it a few weeks before. It had been like pulling teeth getting them done, and I was happy to have that part of it over.

Now, I never was much good with computers and certainly didn't have a real good understanding of how they work. I had no idea that when you saved things on a computer, you were supposed to back up the file to a disk, so that if the computer ever crashed, the information that you had been working on for months wouldn't be lost. I just figured that once the information went into the computer, you would always be able to get it back out, no matter what. After all, the information was going into a box, and logic says that if you put something into a box, you should be able to get it back out. Unfortunately, I was soon to find out that my idea of how computers work is not in any way, shape, or form the same idea that the computer has.

One afternoon we had a pretty bad windstorm that knocked out the power on the ranch. When the power came back on, the computer didn't. Not only did it not come back on, but everything that had been inside it when the power went off was lost to the ages. The notes that I had agonized over all those months had disappeared somewhere inside those tiny little circuits, never to be seen again.

With the date of my speech rapidly approaching, I sat down and tried to recreate my notes. It was no use. The harder I tried to write, the more my mind wandered, until I finally gave up on the idea of talking about troubled horses and began thinking about something else entirely.

The thing that my mind kept coming back to was an idea that I had been playing with for more than twelve years. This idea has to do with what I feel is at the heart of successfully working with horses. It has to do with some of the things we'd done over the years at the ranch where I worked, which enabled us to build a sort of unconditional trust with our herd of around seventy head. I felt that folks might find this subject interesting because, in our search to find ways to gain our herd's trust, we also found that they seemed to look to us as leaders that they willingly sought out and wanted to follow. As a result, we not only ended up with horses that were extremely easy to train, but they were also responsive and dependable, no matter who rode them.

I believe there was one primary reason for the success we had in helping our herd develop that kind of relationship with us—we worked very hard at mimicking the behavior of a certain "lead" horse in the herd. This horse that we chose to mimic was not the "alpha," or dominant horse in the herd, as many folks might suspect. The horse we tried to be most like was a horse with a completely different temperament and role within the herd—a horse that leads by example, not force. A horse that is extremely dependable and confident, one that the vast majority of horses will not only willingly choose to follow, but that they actually seek out.

The biggest obstacle in trying to explain what we did with our herd to the folks at the convention was the fact that, as far as I knew, the type of horse we had tried to mimic didn't have a title. In fact, I had never heard anyone even refer to the horse before. I felt I needed to come up with a term or title for the horse that would best explain its role within the herd. If I could do that, I felt it would make it easier for me to explain why we found it so important to mimic that horse during the work we'd done with our herd.

It took several days, but I finally came up with a title that I thought would best suit this idea, one that I could use when I gave my talk. The title I came up with was "passive leader." Okay, it wasn't very scientific, but it was the best I could do. After all, I *was* running out of time.

At any rate, I chose that title because the horse in question wasn't one that would force its way into the leadership role. Instead, the horse was *chosen* by members of the herd as the one they wanted to follow. The leadership role was bestowed on the horse in a passive way. In other words, it wasn't necessarily looking to be a leader but didn't turn the role down once it had been chosen. The title actually refers to the way the horse is chosen for the role, not to what it does once it's "appointed."

After the convention, I found out that I should have made the idea behind the title a little more clear. As word of my talk spread throughout the horse community, people automatically assumed that in order for our horses to see us as passive leaders, we must treat them in a passive way during training.

This simple misunderstanding caused quite a bit of confusion for a number of folks. Many people couldn't understand how they could possibly get anything done with their horses if they were constantly treating them in a passive manner. After all, the word passive, by definition, means "not acting." How could we possibly train or work with our horses by not acting? Well, the answer to that question is that we can't. Again, the term "passive leader" wasn't designed to illustrate what this particular horse does after he is chosen as leader, but rather *how* he is chosen in the first place.

The question then is, how do we get our horses to want to choose us as a leader? It has been my observation that before a horse (or person) can even be considered as a passive leader, it must first exhibit the qualities that make it desirable for it to be chosen. Those qualities are quiet confidence, dependability, consistency, and a willingness *not* to use force.

What I have tried to do in this book is explain some of the things we found over the years that have helped us attain these qualities in our horse's eyes. By making an effort to establish the qualities that I just mentioned, we quickly found that our horses could put their trust in us. Once we had their trust, it seemed easier for them to look to us as someone they would willingly follow, and even seek out, for leadership and security.

I'm afraid you won't find much information in this book about new or different techniques or what tack or training tools you should use if you try to establish yourself as a passive leader. I have found that tools and techniques don't matter all that much unless they are applied with the right attitude. And, I guess when it comes right down to it, that is what this book is really all about—attitude.

A good friend once told me that she felt that working with horses is like being on a long trip. It's a journey with no destination— an unending process—and everything that is important is "as you go," not "when you get there."

For all of you out there who see horsemanship in that same light, I hope the information that I have tried to share here might help you take one more step in that long journey.

Horses Never Lie

The Question

When I was a kid, I always looked forward to Sunday. Not the entire day, mind you. Mostly just the afternoon, when my parents would load all of us kids in the car and head out for our weekly drive through the country.

"Heading out" into the country didn't mean that much, since we were pretty close to being in the country in the first place. We lived on the outskirts of town on the last paved road before the land opened up into the great expanses of the unknown. At least that was how I looked at it. At eight years old, I considered anything past the corner of Weis and Stow completely uncharted territory. I could stand on that corner and look out across what seemed like thousands of miles of open fields and farmers' pastures. And I could only imagine what kind of scary beasts might lurk out there.

If I looked hard enough, a mile or so away I could see the remains of a barn that had long ago burned down. Or perhaps it had simply fallen down—it was hard to tell. At any rate, the old, deserted house that stood next to the fallen barn was most certainly haunted, and that was reason enough not to venture too far from the safety of the corner.

Except on Sunday. On Sunday we would all climb in the car and drive down the dirt road that went right past that old house. I'll be darned if it didn't look all that bad on Sundays. Particularly when peering at it from the safety of the back seat of a '58 Oldsmobile. Nothing is all that scary when you're surrounded by four tons of glistening steel.

Once past the haunted house, we would take a left onto another dirt road that led us out to the highway. This dirt road was about two miles long, and about halfway down on the right was another deserted ranch. The driveway to the ranch was about a quarter-mile long, and it led up to a couple of run-down barns. There were overgrown pastures on either side of the driveway, all the fences were falling down, and things were in general disrepair. It was a place I never gave much thought to, but one Sunday afternoon that all changed.

On that Sunday we had driven past the haunted house, made our left-hand turn, and were approaching the old ranch when I noticed something out of the ordinary. Horses. There were horses in the ranch's pastures. Not just one or two horses, mind you, but a lot. Perhaps as many as twenty! Maybe even thirty!

As we neared the driveway, I saw that things were definitely different. The ranch didn't look so bad anymore. The fences were fixed, the doors were hung, and the windows had glass in them. In fact, the place actually looked pretty good. Somebody had moved in and cleaned it all up. What's more . . . they brought horses with them!

All my short life I had loved horses. I'm not even sure why. After all, I had never actually been around *real* horses. In fact, the closest I'd ever gotten to a horse was watching Roy Rogers on Trigger, Marshal Dillon on his buckskin, and Joe Cartwright on his paint. So, I have no good explanation as to why I was smitten by them. But like so many other boys and girls my age, I just was.

Having horses that close to my house was way more than I could stand. Even though I had never ventured out that direction on my own before, the draw of real horses within bike-riding distance was worth the risk of being snatched up by the ghosts from the haunted house I'd have to ride past. The very next day I jumped on my bicycle and headed out.

Riding a bike out to that old ranch took a whole lot more time than riding in the Oldsmobile, that's for sure. Seemed like it took forever, except for the little stretch there by the haunted house. That stretch didn't take any time at all. I made sure of that.

At any rate, after what seemed like hours, there I was, standing with my bicycle right in front of the ranch with all those horses grazing quietly in the pastures. Funny, but it wasn't until then that something important dawned on me: *What was I going to do now?* I mean, sure enough, there I was. But why had I gone in the first place? Now that I was there, what was I going to do, turn around and go home? Or stand in the road like an idiot all day long?

It was sad, but true. I had no plan. I guess I had been so worried about just getting there that it never occurred me to wonder *why* I was going or what I was going to do once I got there.

Well, this was going to take some thought. I walked my bike over to the shoulder of the road and slipped it into the deep grass growing wild in the ditch. I sat down next to it and stared out into the pasture at the horses while I tried to formulate a plan. After a bit, with me thinking just as hard as I could, one of the horses raised his head and looked right at me. He was a big, reddish-colored horse with a small white spot on his forehead. A handsome-looking fellow, as I recall. I remember his ears being very erect and his head very high as he stared at me. I sat perfectly still, not wanting to frighten him (and not really knowing what else to do). After a short time, his head began to slowly bob up and down—a peculiar-looking action that I had never seen Trigger do in any of the Roy Rogers movies. He continued the head bobbing for several minutes before he dropped his head and began to make his way slowly toward me.

Well, one thing was certain. I wasn't expecting this. Of all the scenarios I *hadn't* come up with regarding what would happen once I got to the ranch, this was certainly one of them. To say that I was a little nervous about that horse heading my way would be somewhat of an understatement. As the horse approached, I remember thinking, *This is a really big horse!* The closer he got, the faster my heart pounded. Before long, he was standing just on the other side of the fence, and I was in a nervous sweat. I found myself wishing that I had gone to the bathroom before I left the house.

The horse lowered his head to have a good look at me. There was no wind, and the late morning sun was beating down on the two of us. I remember hearing the buzz of flies and the rattle of grasshoppers as they flew here and there. And I remember hearing the horse's breath. It sounded like a person in a deep sleep.

4

Long, relaxed breaths, occasionally punctuated with a little quicker exhale. Each time the horse inhaled, his nostrils got a little bigger. I expect mine did, too.

I continued to sit quietly, being careful not to make any move that might make the horse want to bite, stomp, kick, or otherwise dismember or disembowel me. He responded in kind, staying at a safe distance with the fence between us. After a while, I guess curiosity got the better of both of us. He slowly made his way even closer to the fence. Still a little frightened but getting braver by the minute, I cautiously got to my feet and inched closer to the fence as well.

I had to pass through the deep part of the ditch to get up close to the horse, which I did just as calmly as I could. By the time I'd gotten through the ditch, the horse's head was hanging over the fence, and he was putting his nose out where it was easy for me to touch. I couldn't believe how soft the end of his nose was.

Within minutes, my fear had all but disappeared, and I was making fast friends with the big red horse. He let me pet him on his nose, cheeks, and forehead where that white spot was. In return, I picked some of the waist-high grass and offered it to him. He took it from my hand in polite, almost delicate bites, and while he chewed, I petted.

This went on for quite some time when suddenly I heard an awful racket up by the barn. The horse turned and lazily looked in the direction of the noise, and I had to move a little to my left in order to see what had caused such a disturbance. The sound was coming from an old truck sitting by the barn. Somebody had started the engine and blue smoke was belching from the tail pipe. That could only mean one thing—somebody had seen me and was coming to yell at me for messing with his horse!

I panicked. I turned on my heel and took one hurried stride toward my bike. However, the grass was so deep in the ditch that I couldn't see where it ended and the ground began. As I stepped on what I thought was solid ground, I sunk into the overgrown grass and tripped and fell with a thud on the other side of the ditch. My falling caused the horse to spook and run off, which scared me even more. I scrambled up the other side of the ditch and pulled at my bike, but it had become tangled in the long grass. I pulled and pulled, but it wouldn't come loose. I looked up toward the barn. The truck had turned around and was heading down the driveway right toward me.

I continued to pull, and the truck kept coming my way. Suddenly, with help from a tremendous adrenaline rush, I yanked the bike free. I swung it up on the road and, in one swift and flawless movement, I was on it and pedaling for home. I never looked back, and the truck never caught up with me.

A few days passed before I got up enough nerve to go back out to the ranch. But when I finally did, I went back with a plan. First, I'd make sure that truck wasn't there. If it was, I'd simply turn around and go on back home. If it wasn't there, I'd hide my bike in the ditch and wait for a horse or two to come up to the fence. Once they were at the fence, I'd feed them grass and pet them if they'd let me. It was a good plan and, over the next several weeks, a successful one.

For the rest of the summer I made my way out to the ranch a couple of times a week. Sometimes I'd get to pet horses, sometimes I wouldn't. But either way, I always found the trip worthwhile. If nothing else, I was no longer afraid to go past the haunted house.

The fall, winter, and spring passed without me making too many trips out to the ranch. Too cold to ride a bike that far and too much to do anyway, what with football season in the fall, basketball in the winter, and baseball in the spring. But once summer break rolled around, there I was again, heading back out to the ranch. This time, however, I expanded on my plan. You see, sometimes when I went out to the ranch, the horses would be too far away or in a different pasture altogether. At those times, I wouldn't get to pet any horses, and I considered the trip a waste of time. So, to better my chances of getting to pet the horses on those days, the new plan included trespassing.

From that time forward, if the truck wasn't there and the horses were too far away, I'd crawl through the fence and go to them, instead of waiting for them to come to me. That part of the plan worked great—until one day in late June.

On that particular day, I rode out to the ranch and made sure the truck wasn't anywhere to be seen, which it wasn't. As always, I laid my bike in the ditch and, without hesitation, climbed through the fence and made my way out to the horses. That day they were all up pretty close to the barn, closer than I had ever been. I wasn't worried, though, because the truck wasn't there, which meant the driver of the truck wasn't there either. The truck was so loud that I would hear it coming from at least a mile away and perhaps two or three, if the wind was blowing in the right direction. Plenty of warning for me to get out of the pasture.

By this time the horses all knew me, and I them. They actually seemed glad to see me when I came around and would all gather around me. On that day I was standing with my back to the barn, picking handfuls of grass to feed the horses. Of course, I would pet them all as they took the grass from my hand, and a good time was being had by all.

In retrospect, I probably should have noticed that the horses were occasionally looking past me in the direction of the barn ... as if somebody might have been up there, possibly heading my way. But I didn't notice. You can imagine my surprise when—while petting the horses and jabbering away like a magpie—I suddenly felt the tap of a finger on my shoulder.

I let out a little yell as I spun around. I was shocked to see an old man in a sweat-stained cowboy hat, dirty jeans, and a faded denim shirt. His skin was very dark and weathered, and he had about a week's worth of gray beard. He stood quiet for several seconds just looking at me. It was a concerned gaze that started at my tennis shoes, worked its way up to the top of my head, then went back down to my tennis shoes—as if he were sizing me up for a coffin.

"Whatcha doin'?" he asked, after what seemed like an eternity.

"I ... I'm, uh ... I was ..."

He slowly reached into his shirt pocket and pulled out a pack of filterless Camel cigarettes. He hit the top of the pack several times on the back of his hand, then gave the pack an effortless flick that was enough to force the end of one of the cigarettes out. He nonchalantly took the cigarette between his lips and pulled it the rest of the way out of the pack before returning the pack to his shirt pocket.

"This here's private property," he mumbled, as he reached into his pants pocket and pulled out a tarnished silver lighter.

He flicked open the top of the lighter, ran his thumb over the starter, and in one motion not only had a flame but also had it raised to the end of the cigarette. In less than a second, blue smoke was rolling out of the corner of his mouth.

9

There was no question that I needed to come up with something fast, and before I knew it, I was trying once again to speak.

"I . . . I'm sorry . . ."

The old man closed the cover of the lighter with one hand and slid it back into the watch pocket of his jeans. With his other hand, he took the cigarette from his lips and blew out another puff of smoke. He nodded slowly.

"Well," he said, as he turned and began to walk away, "come on."

Come on? What did he mean, come on? Where was he going? And more importantly, why was I supposed to go along? My next move was something I gave very quick and careful thought to. He had his back to me and was walking away. I could make a break for it! Surely he wouldn't be able to catch me . . . he was old! I was one of the fastest kids on my block. I could outrun him, no problem. A couple steps to my left—enough to give me a little head start—and off I'd go. It was about 200 yards to the fence. I could do that. After all, on top of being old, he smoked! He'd be out of breath before he got halfway to the fence. By that time I'd be on my bike and making tracks. He'd never catch me! It was a good plan. In fact, it was a great plan, and I was just getting ready to implement it when . . .

"You comin'?" he asked, without looking back.

Coming? Why would I want to do that? Surely nothing good would come of it and, in fact, there was a real good chance I could end up dead. No, I needed to make a break for it, and there was no time like the present.

I looked at the fence some 200 yards away, measured my steps, then looked back at the old man as he walked toward the barn. I looked back at the fence, then again at the old man. I was just getting ready to make my break.

"If you're going . . . go on and go," he said, again without looking back. "Otherwise, come on."

It wasn't said in a threatening manner, but in a way that actually relieved some of my nervousness. It was strange, but with that one sentence I suddenly wasn't all that interested in getting away anymore. Probably because he told me I could. Don't get me wrong, I was still plenty apprehensive. Still, I thought maybe it wouldn't be so bad if I went along to see what he had in mind. So, with that, I slowly turned and walked after him as he made his way up to the barn.

On the way, he stopped to open the large wooden gate that separated the pastures. He left it open as he went through, and I passed through, never giving a thought to closing it behind me. The old man stopped dead in his tracks, turned, and looked at the gate. I caught up to him, but even then he continued to look back at the open gate. He took a drag on his cigarette and turned his gaze back to me. He blew the smoke out of his mouth and nose and looked back at the gate.

"Should I close that?" I asked rather sheepishly.

"Whatever you think is best," he replied.

I ran back to the gate, closed it, and latched it. The old man had already continued his trek toward the barn, and I had to run after him to catch up. He reached the barn before I did, went inside, and walked to a nearby wall where several tools and shovels were hanging. Very deliberately he grabbed a large, steel scoop shovel off the wall and handed it to me.

"Here," he said flatly. "If you're gonna pet 'em, you're gonna have to clean up after 'em."

And with that, my career with horses began. Not the most ceremonious of beginnings, I'll grant you, but a beginning nonetheless.

Now, typically, I would seldom, if ever, repeat a story like this. After all, it isn't really much of story when you take it at face value. But sometimes it helps to look past first impressions. Often in life, it isn't the big things that happen to us that have the most profound effect, it's the little things.

I soon found out that the way the old man handled catching me trespassing in his pasture was pretty much the way he handled all situations. Everything he did was low-key, while having a very distinct purpose. His purpose in our first meeting was to accomplish one of two things—either to scare me enough to get me to quit coming around or to open a door for me to come around even more. Either way, the choice was mine.

He worked with horses in much the same way. He would set things up for the horse to make a decision and allow the horse to make it. He never seemed overly concerned about forcing a horse to do something it wasn't comfortable doing or punishing a wrong decision. He would simply let whatever was going to happen, happen, and then go from there. It was a simple idea, but very effective—for both horses and people.

I had been working for the old man for a while, when he purchased a young horse. His story illustrates this idea very well. He was a four-year-old gelding that had been started at eighteen months. As a two year old, he was shown in western pleasure classes with relative success. As a result, his owner decided to show him at every opportunity.

At two and a half, the colt was beginning to grow tired of the rigors of showing and began acting up at inopportune times, usually just before entering the show ring. He had also become hard to catch and was refusing to allow himself to be mounted. By the age of three, his behavior had become so bad that he was sent to a trainer for "straightening out." The trainer was admittedly heavy-handed with the young horse, but the tactics he used seemed, at least for a while, to make the colt behave.

Even so, the young gelding became even more difficult to catch, and he had also taken to biting while being saddled and cinched up. By the age of three-and-a-half, the young horse was once again refusing to enter the show ring, would not allow himself to be shod, and had bolted several times with his owner and his trainer. Each time he ran off with the trainer, he received a severe beating.

By the time the colt had turned four, his owner had given up on him. What's more, the colt had given up on his owner. Figuring that the colt was a lost cause, his owner ran him through a sale, thinking that the killers would buy him and that would be the end of that. But it just so happened that the old man was at the sale and thought the colt might be good for something other than dog meat. He bought the horse for next to nothing, and after getting the colt's history from his previous owner, he brought him home and turned him out in the large pasture with the rest of the herd. The horse soon buddied up with a small group of geldings that always hung together.

It was clear right from the start that "Salty" (as the old man called him due to the specks of white hair on his forehead) was not going to be an easy nut to crack. He was very comfortable with the small band of geldings but would have nothing to do with any person who entered the pasture. If he thought that you might be heading in his direction, he would take off at a dead run for the other end of the pasture. Catching him was definitely out of the question. Oddly enough, that didn't seem to worry the old man. He simply didn't try to catch him.

After Salty had been at the ranch for about three weeks, it was time to rotate the herd to another pasture on the other side of the property. As he always did when it was time to move the herd, the old man went to the gate and yelled, "Come on!" No matter where the horses were, their heads would all pop up, and one by one they'd look in his direction.

"Come on!" the old man would call again. Usually this was all that was needed to get the herd moving in his direction. One more call from the old man and they'd break into a trot. Before you knew it, they would all be standing by the gate. This time was no exception. Less than five minutes from the first call, the entire herd was waiting anxiously by the gate. All of them, that is, except Salty.

Salty had come up with the herd but was standing a safe distance away from the others. The old man and I haltered all the horses, took two or three in each hand, and led them through the gate and over to the other pasture. We did this until Salty was the only horse left in the pasture. He had run away each time one of us tried to approach and now found himself isolated from the herd. We tried several times to get near him, but he was simply not going to have any of it. After about twenty minutes, it became clear that he wasn't going to allow us to get within catching distance of him, much less get a halter on him. The old man slipped the halter under his arm and lit a cigarette.

"Looks like he wants to stay," he said, after taking a long drag. "So, I guess we'll let him."

And with that, we left the pasture. About this time, Salty realized he was alone and he didn't like that one bit. After we left, he came running hell-bent-for-election up to the gate. He was screaming at the top of his lungs and running the fence line right there near the gate. The old man let that go on for about half an hour before going back to the gate with a halter in hand. Salty turned as soon as the old man reached the gate and ran in the other direction for all he was worth. The old man made no effort to go after him but simply turned and went back to what he'd been doing. As soon as he saw the old man retreating, Salty ran back to the gate and once more began calling and pacing.

Another half hour later, the old man went back to the gate, and again Salty ran off. For the rest of the day, the old man continued to give the colt opportunities to be caught. Each time he made the effort, Salty ran off. At the end of the day, Salty was still in the pasture and still calling frantically. That's where we left him for the night.

The next day Salty was still at the gate and still calling. It was clear that he'd had a pretty rough night, as there was a deep rut dug into the ground along the fence line where he had been pacing, and he was covered with dried sweat. The old man approached the gate and, once again, the colt ran off. However, this time he didn't run near as far before he stopped and turned to look at the old man. The old man opened the gate and stood just inside the pasture with halter in hand. The colt watched him carefully but continued to keep his distance. After about ten minutes, the old man turned and left the pasture.

The colt immediately ran up to the gate and began calling. This time the old man stopped and slowly returned to the gate. The colt ran off but stopped after only a few yards. The old man went through the gate and stood inside the pasture. Salty kept his distance.

After about five minutes, the old man turned and was getting ready to leave the pasture when Salty slowly began to make his way over to the gate. This time the old man stopped at the gate and waited. Salty crept toward the old man, stopping a few feet away. The old man made no effort to approach, but rather stood as if waiting for a bus. After waiting a few more minutes, the old man turned as if getting ready to leave and, surprisingly, Salty walked right up to him. The old man turned around very slowly and began gently petting the colt on his shoulder. Soon Salty had allowed himself to be caught and haltered, and the old man led him out of the pasture and over to the rest of the herd.

It was the last time Salty ever refused to be caught.

That's a perfect example of how the old man worked. He put Salty in a position where he needed to make a choice, then simply allowed him to make it. As far as the old man was concerned, there was no right or wrong decision. After all, it didn't make that much difference to him. The one it *would* matter to was Salty. Whatever decision he made, Salty was going to have to live with it. If he didn't like the consequences, it would be up to him to find a way out.

The key to the successful conclusion of this situation, in my opinion, lies in how the old man handled Salty's initial decision. He didn't try to force a different idea on the colt. Instead he showed him that there *could* be a way out—if he wanted it. By repeatedly returning to the pasture, the old man had been, in a sense, telling Salty that he was there for him. He also gave the horse the option of staying where he was or being moved to the pasture with the rest of the herd. In this case, if Salty wanted to make his situation better, he needed help. In order to get that help, Salty first had to put his trust in the old man . . . as he ultimately did.

As time went on, we saw an interesting change in Salty. Before the pasture incident, he had been extremely evasive and somewhat defensive. Afterwards, he gradually made less and less effort to run away when someone came around. He even seemed to become genuinely interested in people. In a few short weeks, he made an effort to stand still and allow people to approach and pet him—something that was out of the question when he first arrived.

When it came time to move the herd again a few weeks later, the old man went to the gate and called for the horses. They all came running. Salty allowed himself to be caught and moved without incident, and from that point on, he was easy and even fun to be around. The interesting thing (well, at least it's interesting to me) is that no specific "training technique" was used to make this change in him. It just happened.

But I believe that was how the old man looked at working with horses. I guess he just figured that sometimes the less you do, the more you can accomplish. That was certainly the case with Salty, as well as many other horses that had the benefit of being at the old man's little horse operation.

———

Since that time I have run into a great many horse people who have just the opposite idea about how horses should be worked. Basically, they believe that if the horse isn't doing what you want it to do, you must find a way to *make* the horse do it. As you can imagine, having grown up a certain way, it was very hard for me to understand why someone would find this idea beneficial. Not that there is anything necessarily wrong with the idea, mind you. It's just that it seemed foreign to me.

This idea of *making* the horse perform ties directly into another idea or theory that was introduced to me a number of years ago and that I also had a lot of trouble understanding. It was then, and still is, a very popular belief that, in order for a horse to work well for you during training, that horse must first see you as the "alpha" horse of the herd. In other words, your horse must see you as the dominant member of his herd no matter what, and he must submit to you in all situations.

I don't mind telling you that this was an idea that bothered me right from the get-go, and at first I didn't even know why. All I knew was that it didn't sound right to me. As a result, I looked for someone who could either explain it to me or show me what was meant by becoming the alpha.

As luck would have it, I ran across a trainer who was a self-proclaimed expert on the subject. He told me that the best way to have your horse see you as the alpha is for you to be the one who "doesn't move your feet" during training. He went on to demonstrate by teaching a green horse how to longe for the first time. He stood in the middle of a round pen and, with the horse on a long line, began cracking a whip behind him. The horse became confused and extremely nervous. At one point, the colt nearly jumped in the guy's lap trying to get away from the noise of the whip.

Undaunted, the trainer continued to point his finger in the direction he wanted the colt to go and cracked the whip behind him. True to his word, the trainer refused to move his feet during the training session. The horse responded by moving his feet (but not in any particular direction) and more than once got himself tangled in the long line.

Nearly ten minutes into the session, the horse finally figured out what was being asked of him and began traveling in a counterclockwise direction around the trainer. Unfortunately, he made only one revolution before he stopped dead in his tracks and turned toward the trainer. The trainer cracked the whip once again, and the horse jumped into action, running wildly around the pen. It took several more stops and several more cracks of the whip before the horse finally figured out that stopping wasn't an option.

Shortly after that, the trainer turned and faced me. With a smile on his face, he stood perfectly still as the colt traveled around him in an even trot. Each time the colt passed behind him, the trainer switched the rope from one hand to the other behind his back but barely acknowledged the horse's presence in any other way.

"See," he said, knowingly. "This is what it means to be the alpha. He's working and I'm not. It's really pretty simple when you get the hang of it."

Following this demonstration, the trainer took me around his place to show me some of his horses. We walked into a pen where five or six horses were kept and, as if on cue, they all turned and walked away from us. I found this troubling, as I had always been around horses that liked to be near people. Admittedly, the horses I'd been around wouldn't always come running up when someone entered their pen, but they never turned and walked away, either. This display raised some questions for me, and I asked the trainer if this was a common occurrence with his horses.

"Yeah," he replied with a smile, "but watch this."

With that, he took the lead rope he was carrying and slapped the end of it on the ground several times. The horses all jumped, ran off several steps, and then turned around in unison to face him.

"They know what side their bread is buttered on," he said with a grin.

There was no question that the horses knew what it meant when that lead rope hit the ground. The sad thing, at least from my perspective, was the look of resignation in all the horses' eyes. It's something that's hard to explain, but they all looked hollow—as if they weren't even there. They all stood with heads low and ears back and gave the occasional flick of the tail.

That wasn't at all the look the old man got from the horses on his place. His horses always seemed willing and friendly and seldom, if ever, did they walk away from you when you entered their pen. At that point, I knew I had been witness to two completely different styles of handling horses. The old man's style of handling them, and this "new" way of handling them where the person took on the role of the alpha horse.

Over the next several years, I watched many people who considered themselves the alpha, and I came to realize that there are actually two ways people have of becoming the alpha during training. The first is a total domination of the horse at all times, both while riding and while working on the ground. The second is a sort of partial domination, in which force is used in response to an unwanted or negative reaction that the trainer gets from the horse.

Where total domination is used, it's not uncommon to see a trainer use spurs, whips, crops, a loud voice, and a heavy hand at all times, even when they aren't warranted. What I notice in the horses handled this way is that they seem to respond out of fear. There's no question that they do what they're told, but they don't do it willingly. These horses often become hard to handle or angry and defensive, and they sometimes develop reputations as "problem" horses. Very often, these are the horses that quit their riders at the most inopportune time, when the riders need them the most.

One horse that fits this mold sticks out in my memory. He was a young performance horse whose trainer used a pretty heavy hand on him. Now, this trainer prided himself on being the horse's "dominant herd leader" and made a point every chance he got to let the horse know that he was superior to the horse in every way. If the horse wouldn't allow himself to be caught, the trainer ran him mercilessly until he gave in. Once caught, the trainer backed the horse by shaking and jerking heavily on the lead rope until the colt backed a sufficient distance at a sufficient speed. The trainer then led the horse away, and if the horse got too close, he once again jerked and shook the lead rope, yelling "Back!" and backing him as far as he thought was necessary to make his point. If the horse lagged behind, the trainer would go to his side and slap the horse repeatedly on the rump with the end of the lead rope, forcing the horse in a circle around him. When the trainer figured the horse was responding appropriately, they could continue on their way.

During saddling, the horse was expected to stand perfectly still. If he didn't, there was hell to pay in the form of heavy jabs in the belly with the trainer's thumb and more jerks on the lead rope. Once saddled, the trainer would take the horse to the round pen and proceed to longe him for at least twenty minutes. He was expected to walk, trot, lope, and stop flawlessly, while the trainer shouted commands from the middle of the pen. A mistake on the horse's part warranted quick retribution from the trainer and further drilling until the response was acceptable in the trainer's eyes.

Once mounted, the colt was expected to stand perfectly still until he was asked to move. When he was asked to move, the transitions upward were to be flawless—from a perfect standstill to a walk, trot, or lope with no hesitations. If an upward transition were sluggish, the trainer would bring his spurs and the ends of the reins into play and work until the transition was acceptable. He would use the same technique on the horse if his spins weren't quite up to par. Stops were also expected to be flawless. If a stop wasn't perfect, the trainer would put the colt in a little bigger bit and slide him into a wall or fence. Eventually, the stop would no longer be flawed.

After a few months of training, the horse's reactions and responses, while extremely mechanical, were certainly good enough to begin his career in the show arena, and he was taken to several small- and medium-sized reining competitions. He actually did pretty well, taking home second- and third-place finishes in the majority of his starts.

After a while the colt had done so well that the trainer decided to step him up in competition and began taking him to some bigger shows. The gelding did relatively well in his first two competitions, and a number of buyers began to show interest in him. But in his third major competition, with the prospective buyers in attendance, problems arose.

In the practice pen, the trainer was having a hard time getting solid stops from the colt, and his transitions weren't much better. The gelding was refusing to do his flying lead changes, and his spins were slow and lifeless. The trainer, evidently upset with the colt's lackluster behavior, ended up working him over pretty good there in the practice pen and was finally able to get the type of performance he'd been looking for.

But it was the colt that was to have the final say on how that day ended up. You see, when it came time to enter the arena to run his pattern, the colt entered quietly, but then, out of the blue, pitched one of the biggest fits that anybody in three counties had ever seen. He bogged his head and went to bucking like he was at the National Finals Rodeo in Las Vegas.

To his credit, the trainer was able to stay on for the first three or four jumps, but I think he may have regretted it afterwards. Those were some of the hardest jumps anyone remembered seeing (particularly in a reining competition), and most folks couldn't figure out who was squealing the loudest—the horse, as he bellered with every jump, or the trainer as he came down first on the cantle of the saddle, then on the saddle horn, and finally on the horse's neck.

At any rate, the trainer ended up in a heap in the dirt with a smashed hat and ripped jeans, and the colt made three exuberant laps around the arena, running, bucking, and passing gas all the way. The pair were politely excused from running their pattern that day, and the prospective buyers seemed to lose interest in both the horse and the trainer.

So, at least in this particular situation, becoming the horse's "dominant herd leader" didn't really have the positive end result that the trainer had hoped for. The horse, on the other hand, may have had a different opinion. I expect he figured that it ended just as it should have.

———

Now, there is another way that people become the leader or alpha in their horse's "herd." It's actually the more common method and seems to be taught on a larger scale by a great number of trainers. The basic premise is still to have the horse see you as the dominant leader, but to also make more of an effort to see things from the horse's perspective. At least that's the idea. Where I've seen this method used, the practical application seems very similar to that of the trainer and the reining horse. The result in the horse (while things don't usually end with the horse bucking its rider off during an important show) is similar in a lot of respects. The horse performs without much "feel," seeming more like a machine than a truly willing partner.

I've seen horses trained by an owner acting as the alpha that simply detach themselves from the entire process. That isn't to say that they don't perform for the owner, because they do. In fact, on the surface they often seem to perform flawlessly. However, they aren't always consistent in their performance and they aren't very happy when they do perform. In fact, one time they may perform the task without any hesitation and the next time they may not even try. It's pretty common for a horse like this to regularly try to tell its rider that it isn't happy with this type of relationship. The horse communicates this in a number of ways, including hollow-looking eyes, ears held back, tail constantly wringing, and refusal to perform. In some cases, the horse becomes hard to catch, even after extensive time has been spent teaching it how to be caught.

Now, before I go any further, it is important for me to say that there is absolutely nothing wrong with this idea or style of training. And I mean *absolutely* nothing wrong with it. Not all horses trained in such a way develop the behavioral or attitudinal problems that I just described. Rather, I think it's simply a personal preference—a method of training that either works for people and their horses or it doesn't. I believe it comes down to the type of relationship you're looking for with your horse. If you want your horse to see you as the alpha or dominant herd leader, then that is what you should pursue. Many, many trainers and horse owners have a tremendous amount of success working with horses in such a way and, in fact, some horses do prefer to be handled in such a way.

However, I also believe, after watching many horses with riders who have used that method, that this type of relationship is very often less of a partnership between two individuals and more of a dictatorship. Sort of, "I say, you do."

Personally, I would rather have my horse see me as more of a partner than a dictator. More like, "Let's do this together." That was the attitude that was so prevalent at the old man's little horse operation. When someone needs to step up and be the leader, I can do that. But not in a way where the horse sees it as domineering or disrespectful of it and what it is.

Thinking back to how the old man worked with his horses, he always had a very easy-going air about him. That wasn't to say that he would let horses have the run of the place or that he didn't expect them to behave themselves and have decent manners. But he also made a big effort to allow them to have their say in everything being asked of them. He would listen to them, take their point of view into consideration, and go from there. As a result, all his horses were extremely consistent, willing, quiet, and responsive.

Maybe it's just like old Salty. He decided not to allow himself to be caught. As far as the old man was concerned, so be it. However, Salty had to live with his decision and its consequences, which he soon found were somewhat less than desirable. When he tried to find a way out of the situation, the old man was right there for him ... but the decision was all Salty's to make. When given the opportunity, he chose on his own what was right for him in the long run, and no real training intervention was needed. The old man found a way to give Salty his dignity while accomplishing the goal at the same time.

Perhaps that's the secret of how the old man worked with horses. Perhaps that one little thing was the single most important part of the way he worked with horses—being able to accomplish a goal without demeaning the horse or forcing his ideas on it and, in return, having the horse *want* to do things for him. He allowed the right decision to truly be that of the horse and was not overly concerned with a wrong decision. Either way, maybe it shouldn't make all that much difference to any of us.

I don't mind telling you that it certainly makes me wonder, though. If horses are supposed to respond positively to trainers becoming the alpha of the herd, why do so many horses have such trouble with the idea? Is there something that we're missing? Is there something that we aren't doing correctly during training?

The answers to these questions eluded me for an awful long time, and yet the idea of becoming the herd leader continued to eat at me. It finally dawned on me that perhaps I wasn't asking the right questions in the first place. Maybe the question I should be asking was something I had missed altogether. You see, I had been viewing the entire situation from my perspective—as a person looking at a horse. In order to look at it from my horse's perspective, I needed to truly understand how he sees his relationship with the alpha of the herd. Is that a relationship he likes and is happy with? Is the alpha a horse in the herd that he looks up to, respects, and follows willingly? Or is it a horse that he would rather not be around in the first place?

Over the next several years, with the help and patience of numerous horses and people alike, the answers to those questions finally started to become a little clearer for me.

I soon found out that they were already pretty clear to the horses.

NOTES FOR THE QUESTION

It has always been my contention that working with horses is, or at least should be, a delicate balancing act between finding how much or how little direction it will take to help the horse we are working with understand whatever it is we are trying to teach. Too little direction and our efforts might become ineffective. Too much direction and we may develop resistance and animosity between our horse and us.

I recall back when I wrote this book there was a big push in many horsemanship circles for the person working with the horse to become the "alpha" in the horse's eyes—the boss horse. This push seemed to be picking up a lot of steam and as a result I was beginning to see a lot of resentful horses and just as many frustrated owners. I guess the reason for that was that for many people, becoming the alpha also translated into having to bring up emotion such as anger when they were trying to get their horse to do something, and this in turn often translated into the arbitrary use of force. In many cases, neither the horse or the person understood this use of force very well and as a result, people were ending up with problems after a training session that were much bigger than the ones they started with.

The delicate balance and subtle nuances that can be horsemanship were beginning to get lost in all the whacking and pushing that was being taught in order for the human to become the alpha. In writing this chapter, I wanted to slow things down a little and begin to lay a foundation in which people who were following, or thinking of following, the "alpha" philosophy could compare what they were hearing or perhaps doing with a slightly different path ...

a path in which things could become a little more balanced, both in the way we handle our horses and in the way they responded.

The Nature of the Herd

I was just about finished cleaning the box stall when the old man walked past. Without saying a word, he motioned for me to follow him. That usually meant he had something very important for me to do, or at least something more important than what I was doing at the time. So I leaned the scoop shovel against the wall and headed out the back door of the barn. By the time I got out, he'd already walked over to one of the corrals just to the side of the barn. He was leaning against the fence, looking out into the large pasture on the other side of the corral.

He looked like something was on his mind or as though he had something really important to tell me. Perhaps he was upset with the way I was cleaning the stalls. Or maybe he'd found out that I had scratched his saddle the day before, even though I rubbed the scratch out. Perhaps he was just fed up with me being around and was going to let me go. It was hard to say. Whatever it was, it was more important than finishing the stall that I had been cleaning, which probably meant it was bad news.

I walked over and stood next to him. He was lighting a cigarette as I reached the fence, and he took a long drag before putting the lighter back in his pocket and propping his foot up on the bottom rail. He took the cigarette from his mouth and lightly blew smoke out as he exhaled. He was still looking out into the pasture, but I expected something momentous was about to be said and I kept my eyes on him.

I suppose about thirty seconds had passed before it was clear he wasn't going to say anything after all and that whatever he'd brought me out of the barn for was in the pasture, not in the corral. I scanned the pasture for something out of the ordinary—a fence that was down, a gate that had been left open, or something that didn't look right—but I couldn't see anything. I looked back at the old man, and this time he motioned for me to look at the pasture again.

Suddenly something caught my eye. It was close to the ground in the middle of the pasture, some seventy-five yards away. The horses had grazed the pasture down so the grass was only about ankle high. This helped, and I saw two adolescent rabbits playing in the sun. There was a third, much larger rabbit lazily nibbling grass nearby, apparently oblivious to the younger two.

Surely this wasn't what the old man had taken me away from my work for. It was certainly a fun thing to watch, but wasn't it just a little bit of a waste of time? After all, I had stalls to clean. I looked back at the old man in a questioning manner. Without taking his eyes off the activity, he motioned for me to turn my attention back to the rabbits.

By this time those two younger rabbits were really getting after it. One would chase the other, catching and tackling it before they both jumped clear out of the grass and ran in a large circle just as fast as they could go. It was a very high-energy game of tag, but I was still confused as to why I had been asked to watch.

After about five minutes, the pair had ventured quite a ways from the bigger rabbit and seemed to be running out of steam. They were still chasing each other, but without nearly the speed or enthusiasm of just a few minutes earlier. Then, as if someone had flipped a switch, they both stopped dead in their tracks and just stood looking at one another. Even at the distance we were from them, we could see their little bodies expanding very rapidly with each breath they took.

In a flash, something else caught my eye. It was in the tall grass just on the other side of the pasture. It looked like a large, gray dog lying on its belly; it was staring intently at the two rabbits. All my attention had been focused on the rabbits, and I had completely missed the fact that a coyote had crept up. I looked up at the old man, who had also seen the coyote. He seemed unfazed by the fact that something pretty bad was about to happen to those little rabbits.

As I looked back to the pasture, the coyote burst from his hiding spot and went right after them. The older rabbit was gone in a second, disappearing into a nearby hole in the ground. The young ones made a desperate dash for the hole as well, but one didn't make it. Obviously exhausted from their earlier play, the rabbit simply didn't have enough gas in its tank to outrun the coyote.

31

As the coyote trotted off with its prize, the old man crushed his cigarette out on the fence post.

"I guess he shoulda been more careful."

And with that, he simply turned and walked away, leaving me to contemplate the entire situation.

Now, knowing that the old man never did anything without a reason, it was up to me to figure out not only the significance of what he'd just shown me, but also how it would apply to me. At first glance, it seemed that this episode had no correlation whatsoever with anything that was going on at the time. It wouldn't take long, however, before I found out just how wrong I was.

You see, for the past couple of weeks I'd been working with a seven-year-old mare named Star. She was very kind-hearted and gentle and had only one small problem. She was one of the laziest horses I'd ever been around. The old man had owned her for quite some time, but he never really used her for much. For the most part, she just stood in the pasture all day.

One day he decided out of the blue that we were going to start getting her in shape so he could sell her. On the first day I worked with her, he went out and rode her before having me get on, and she was a perfect little lady for him. She did absolutely everything he asked of her without hesitation, from flawless transitions to flying lead changes, sliding stops, side passing, and backing all the way across the arena. After watching him, I couldn't wait to get on and ride, as I had been assigned the task of giving her daily exercise. Well, my enthusiasm quickly waned as I found that I could barely get her from a walk to a trot. As the weeks went on, I found myself increasingly discouraged by the fact that I was lucky if I could even get her into a walk from a standing stop.

A few days following the rabbit incident, I was in the arena, trying with all my might to get the mare to work for me. We had been going around and around the arena barely faster than a crawl, with me kicking her repeatedly and slapping her with the reins to try to get her to move a little faster. Nothing I did got any kind of reaction from her, with the exception of the occasional tail flick or head shake. As we made our way around the arena at sloth-like speed, I noticed that the old man was at the fence watching the proceedings.

"How's it going?" he asked, as a snail whizzed passed Star and me in the dirt of the arena.

"I can't get her to do nothin'," I told him in disgust.

He nodded slowly and placed his foot on the bottom rail of the fence. Star, seeing the old man, suddenly picked up her pace and headed straight for him, stopping within arms' reach. The old man put his hand out and stroked her gently on the forehead.

"This is the laziest horse I've ever seen," I told him, drawing that conclusion from the vast experience of all the five or six horses I had worked to that point.

He smiled as he continued to pet the mare on her head.

"Lazy, eh," he nodded, as if he was agreeing, but I knew he wasn't. "Oh, I don't think she's being lazy. Smart, maybe. But not lazy."

"Smart?" I questioned. "I don't think she's very smart. I think she's stupid."

It was frustration talking, and the old man knew it. It didn't matter though. He didn't like people calling his horses names. He slowly stopped petting the mare, then looked up at me with an expression that said, *That'll be enough of that.* Without saying a word, he turned and walked through the gate and motioned for me to get down, which I gladly did.

Without stopping to adjust the stirrups, he climbed into the saddle, turned the mare's head to the left, kissed to her, and they were off. Much to my chagrin she went from a standing stop to a lope without missing a step. At the other end of the arena, she slid to a stop, spun on her back end, and was once again in a lope. The old man, reins in one hand and feet out of the stirrups, looked like he was glued to the saddle. The two flew past me and slid to another stop before reversing once more and heading back the other way. This time, about halfway across the arena, the old man shifted his weight slightly backwards in the saddle and the mare went from her lope to a slow walk within about three steps. He leaned forward and she was back in a lope. They loped all the way around the arena; as they rounded the corner closest to me, they broke down into a trot, then a walk, and finally a stop, right next to me.

It was the first and only time I ever saw the old man "show off" while riding a horse, or when doing anything, for that matter. It was obvious that he hadn't done it to show me how good a rider he was, but to show me how good a horse Star was. As the old man climbed down, the mare was stood quietly next to him, and both of them were looking at me as if to say, *Stupid, huh?*

"Now," he said quietly, as he handed me the reins, "why don't you try again?"

"She won't do that for me." Even I could hear the resignation in my voice. The old man continued to hold the reins out to me.

"You're right," he said, with a shrug. "If you think she won't, she won't. Maybe it's time you start thinking that she will."

Well, that didn't make any sense at all, and as I took the reins from his hand and climbed into the saddle, confusion and frustration must have been written all over my face. He walked over to the fence and pulled out his pack of cigarettes.

35

"There's something about horses that you need to under-stand," he said, as he rolled the nearly empty pack between his fingers until he had worked the last cigarette to the opening. He pulled the cigarette out, crumpled the empty pack, and put it in his jeans pocket.

"Horses are a lot like them rabbits we saw the other day." He pulled out his lighter and quickly lit the end of the cigarette hanging from his lips. "Their only real job in this world is to stay alive from one day to the next. Nothing else really matters."

He went on to explain that the reason horses (or any prey animal, for that matter) had survived as a species was because they're smart enough to know when to expend energy and when not to. He used the rabbits as an example.

"Them two young rabbits was out playing in the sun," he said, as he leaned up against the fence. "They ran until they got tired. The bad thing was that they had used up so much of their energy playing that they didn't have any left for when they really needed it." He took a drag from the cigarette. "Now, if every rabbit from the beginning of time used that much energy during the day, we wouldn't have any rabbits, would we? They'd all be dead by now."

Okay, what on earth did this have to do with the mare not wanting to work for me? I felt sure he was making a point, but I couldn't see what it was. My confusion must still have been pretty evident, because normally in a situation like this he would have left it at that and let me figure out what he was talking about on my own. Instead, he continued to explain.

"For this horse to want to work for you, the work has to be important to her. If it isn't important to her, you're just making her use energy she doesn't think she should be using. She might need that energy later to get away from a lion or wolf or bear."

"There aren't any lions or wolves or bears around here," I told him bluntly.

"She doesn't know that," he replied with a smile. "She's just looking out for herself."

He went on to say that no amount of training in the world can take away what Mother Nature has instilled. Just because we think a horse should do things a certain way doesn't mean that the horse sees it the same way. In this case, Star was just letting me know that I couldn't make her perform a meaningless task that would cause her to use energy she might need later.

"So," the old man said, "what we need to do is find a way to make what you want to do important enough so that she wants to do it with you."

"Great," I said, with a hint of sarcasm. "How do I do that?"

Without saying it straight out, he let me know the first thing I needed to do was lose the attitude—which I took to heart. He told me that the way I was riding had a lot to do with how Star had perceived the situation. He explained that I was riding without purpose or direction. Up to that point I had been demanding that she go, but not giving her any place to go.

He pointed out that the whole time I was hitting her with the reins and kicking her in the sides to try to get her to move faster, I was also staring straight at her head. By looking at her instead of where I wanted to go, I wasn't giving her any direction. Her perception was that I had left the direction up to her, and seeing as how Mother Nature geared her to save as much energy as possible throughout the day, she took it upon herself to do what Mother Nature was telling her, not what I was telling her.

It turns out that by constantly staring at the mare's head in such a way, I was actually riding in a sort of ball. My head was down, which brought my upper body forward and rounded my shoulders. As far as Star was concerned, my body had the feel of a giant, uncomfortable lump that she had been relegated to packing around. There was no "togetherness" in how I was riding; I was simply riding on the mare, not with her.

The old man had me sit up a little straighter in the saddle and focus on where I wanted to go. Almost immediately I could feel a difference in her, even as we just stood in place. Her head came up and her attention seemed more focused on me than it ever had before.

"There," he said. "Now look over to the other end of the arena and pick a post, then ride to it. Don't take your eyes off that post."

I turned my head and looked to the other end of the arena. At the middle of the turn was a post that was a little bigger than the rest. I focused on that post, then took the reins and laid them across her neck to help turn her in that direction. She responded right away, and when I kissed to her just like the old man had, off she went. To my surprise, her walk was much quicker than it had been for the past two weeks, and I could feel my excitement begin to build at the thought of actually being able to move faster than our normal crawl. I kissed to her again and her walk quickened.

I couldn't believe how well she was working all of a sudden, and from behind me I heard the old man ask me to move her up into a trot. I kissed to her and squeezed lightly with my heels and, just like that, she was trotting. Another kiss and squeeze and we were into one of the nicest lopes I had ever felt. I was still watching the post, but pretty quick we were reaching the end of the arena.

"Just ask her to come back around, then pick another post on this end and ride to it," the old man called.

I turned my head to look to the other end of the arena, and she began to make a very smooth turn in the direction I was looking. I picked another post at the other end of the arena and rode to it. She never missed a beat and continued in her nice, even lope all the way to where the old man stood. I gently picked up on the reins and she came to a quiet stop just a few feet from him.

"There," he said, as he nodded his head ever so slightly. "That's the difference between riding on her and riding with her."

The mechanics of what we had done weren't difficult to understand. It was a matter of not expecting the horse to do the work if I wasn't willing to do it with her. By showing her with my body position and attitude in the saddle that I actually had a clue as to what I was doing, the work became important to both of us (even if it was just going across the arena).

At the time, I was so excited about the progress I'd made with the mare that day that a big part of what the old man had said completely escaped me. It was the reason she hadn't been working in the first place—the part about her needing to save her energy in case of a real crisis, during which she'd need it. That one thing may be the single most important part of working with horses, and I almost missed it.

When all this happened with Star, I guess I wasn't more than twelve or thirteen years old. As a young person, the idea of death or dying was the farthest thing from my mind. The whole concept is lost on the majority of young people because, for the most part, they feel physically and mentally invincible. And if they are invincible, why shouldn't everything and everybody else be, too?

So, when the old man spoke about how horses are geared to save energy in case they need to get away from a predator, I really didn't get it. After all, death was something that just didn't happen.

And besides, all of the big predators had long since been trapped or hunted out of the area anyway. So what did the horses have to worry about? What I didn't realize was that he wasn't just talking about the horses at his little ranch, but every horse on the planet. It's a survival mechanism in the horse that has not evolved out of them, and may not ever. It's quite possibly the most important thing in the horse's make-up that has kept the species alive all these millions of years. And, while this need to conserve energy is certainly more prevalent in some horses than others, it is definitely something that is common to them all.

Once I finally came to that understanding, it was evident that there was more to this "survival" thing than met the eye. What I mean is that horses will go to seemingly extraordinary lengths to ensure not only their own survival, but the survival of the species. By the same token, it is often these survival tactics that we misconstrue as the horse being belligerent, troublesome, or lazy.

For instance, several years ago I was working as a wrangler for a large dude operation. This operation had over 115 horses that were used daily for the sole purpose of taking people on trail rides. These horses were very well cared for in every way. They were meticulously groomed each day; wore tack that fit well; were grained twice a day; fed an excellent-quality hay at night; and were handled in a kind manner by all the wranglers. In return, most of the horses seemed to enjoy their work and didn't seem to mind the drudgery of walking the same trails day after day.

There was one horse in the string, however, that didn't quite fit the mold. Kit was a ten-year-old mare that was extremely quiet, and she was used almost exclusively as a kid's horse. She never acted up, always stayed in line, seldom tried to steal bites of grass along the trail like many of the other kid's horses did, and went about her business without much fanfare. The only problem with Kit was that she was slow. Now when I say she was slow, I mean she was really slow. She was so slow, in fact, that sometimes it was hard to tell if she was moving at all. As a wrangler you always knew that if Kit was on one of your rides, it was pretty much a given that you would be getting back to the barn anywhere from fifteen minutes to half an hour late. As a result, most of us had devised shortcuts that would cut up to a quarter mile off the original trail just so we could get back on time. These soon became known as "Kit trails."

Because she was so slow, the boss hesitated to use Kit very much. But on the other side of the coin, she was such a good horse in every other respect that he couldn't see fit to get rid of her. She may have been slow, but she was also very safe and quiet, just the kind of horse you want for inexperienced kids going on their first trail ride.

At one point, one of the wranglers had just about had enough of Kit's snail-like behavior on the trail and decided to work with her and teach her how to walk faster. The wrangler got on Kit and began kicking and slapping her with the reins, much like I had done with Star all those years before. It was clear that the wrangler had the same attitude in the saddle that I had had with Star. She was balled up in the saddle and staring straight down at Kit's head. Kit responded by putting one foot in front of the other so slowly that it almost appeared she was going backwards. After about five minutes of this, the wrangler became pretty agitated. She jumped off, tied Kit to the hitch rail, and headed off to the bunkhouse to retrieve her spurs.

As she strode back toward Kit, the boss noticed the spurs strapped to her boots and stopped her. The wrangler explained how she'd been working with Kit to try to teach her how to move faster but hadn't had much luck. She'd decided she'd use the spurs on her and hopefully teach her a lesson.

"You don't need spurs on that mare," the boss said. He walked over and untied Kit from the hitch rail. He climbed on, turned her head, gave a nudge with his heels, and off she went. They loped effortlessly across the yard, around a tree, up a little hill, and back to the wrangler. The boss climbed down off Kit and handed the reins to the wrangler.

"You don't have to teach her how to go faster. She already knows how," he told her. "She's just got this deal figured out."

He was right. Kit had figured out how to do the least amount of work possible and still keep her job. I believe she understood that the faster she got back to the barn, the quicker she would be going out on another ride, and thus the more work she would be doing. On the other hand, if she walked slow enough, she not only successfully slowed the entire ride down to her pace, but she short-ened the amount of time she had to work in any given day. She had also succeeded in causing the wranglers to shorten up the trails she took. So, even when she was being used, she was actually working less than other horses.

Talk about finding ways to conserve energy! Kit was a master at it. She had found little things in her situation that she could use to her best interest, and thus found a way to alter her "surroundings" to fit her particular needs.

Now I'm sure there are a number of folks who would say that horses aren't smart enough to figure something like that out. You know, maybe those folks are right. But what if they're wrong? What if horses can figure those kinds of things out? What if they can think that far ahead?

Here's another example of horses thinking ahead in a situation. It's a simple thing and is extremely common. I'm talking about horses that bloat when you tighten the cinch. Most horse folks run into a horse with this problem from time to time. Usually the horse has been repeatedly cinched so tight that it caused major discomfort. To eliminate the anticipated discomfort, the horse expands its chest cavity while the cinch is being tightened. Once the cinch has been tightened, the horse allows its chest cavity to return to normal size, and the cinch is acceptably snug . . . in the horse's eyes.

While this is an annoying habit for the rider, it is also avoidable. If the cinch hadn't been tightened to the point where the horse felt the need to defend itself, the problem would have never started in the first place. To me, the interesting thing is that horses all over the world have figured out how to help themselves in this situation. Nobody taught them how to expand their chests to relieve the discomfort. They figured it out on their own.

Thousands, perhaps millions, of horses have independently come to the same solution on how to "fix" a cinch that is too tight. It seems to me that this is a clear case of self-preservation in a sort of passive way. The horse is defending itself without relying on physical force. It's an attempt to avoid conflict, if you will, while at the same time accomplishing that which is in the horse's own best interest.

The more I'm around horses, the easier it is to see that—for the most part—that's just how they are. They seem to want nothing more than to get through the day with the least amount of conflict and strife possible, while doing everything in their power to keep themselves safe from harm. They always seem to be a making a conscious effort to look for ways to help themselves accomplish that goal.

This brings me back to Kit. When the day was over at the dude ranch, the entire herd of over 115 horses was turned out on about ten acres of dry-lot pasture. There they would spend the night and there they were fed their hay—nearly three tons per day. As soon as the hay was dumped into the feeders, minor fights broke out amongst the horses. But to say that these were fights isn't quite accurate. They were more a series of scuffles between "boss" horses exerting their dominance over the "lower" horses of the herd, telling them when and where they could eat.

Kit was seldom involved in the fights and would stand off by herself until all the hay was fed and the horses had settled into their respective feeders. Then, and only then, would she pick the feeder with the fewest horses around it, go over, and begin eating. Seldom, if ever, did she end up in a fight.

As the weeks went on, I noticed a very interesting thing begin to happen at feeding time. Instead of all of the horses running up to the feeders as soon as the hay was doled out, three or four were staying back near Kit. Once the dust had settled and all the others were eating, Kit would pick the feeder with the fewest horses around it and walk over to it. The horses that had waited with her followed as if she was a magnet. At the feeder Kit chose, there was no fighting and all the horses seemed to get along just fine. A few weeks later, another three or four horses had joined Kit. By midsummer there were eight or ten horses that followed her everywhere she went. If she walked to the water, they all walked to the water. If she stood in the shade, they all stood in the shade. If she ate, they all ate.

Kit was unfazed by her popularity and appeared to accept the others as if they had been buddies all their lives. The little band that followed her never seemed to get into arguments, living in relative peace whenever they were all together.

As the summer went on, other bands similar to the one that had formed around Kit began to pop up within the herd. In each band the horses willingly chose one horse out of the bunch as a sort of leader. The one chosen by the others was usually very similar to Kit in demeanor and temperament—they were quiet, unassuming, and very consistent in their behavior.

In contrast, there were other, much smaller bands of horses within the herd where quiet and consistency were completely non-existent. These horses were continually in turmoil, fighting and chasing one another from one day to the next.

Now, over time it became apparent that the herd of over 115 horses was split into two distinct sections, best described as the "haves" and the "have-nots." The "haves" were the horses that were clearly in charge, although they weren't many in number, perhaps only ten or twelve. These were the boss horses or alphas, I guess you could call them—the horses that always ate first, always drank first, and were always at the gate first thing in the morning so they could get into the barn to get their grain first. The rest—the "have-nots"—all ranked much further below the "haves," even though they outnumbered them nearly ten to one.

The interesting thing about this setup was the distinct contrast in the behavior of the two camps. The majority of the herd, the "have-nots," seldom challenged one another for any reason. That's not to say that it didn't happen, because it did. It's just that it wasn't a very common occurrence. When it came to feeding time or getting a drink of water, the majority seemed content to wait their turn and, in some cases, even seemed polite, as one would allow another to butt in line at the water tank or feed trough.

The "haves," on the other hand, were quite willing to start trouble any chance they got. Butting in line wasn't an option when one of these horses was at the water tank or feed trough. In fact, simply passing a little too close to one of these horses could result in an all-out attack on the hapless "have-not." As a result, the "haves" spent the majority of their time causing turmoil within the herd by constantly exerting their dominance, and the "have-nots" seemed to spend the majority of their time avoiding them. The resulting separation within the herd was quite clear. The "haves" pretty much stuck to themselves, and so did the "have-nots."

Since that time I've had the opportunity to oversee quite a few large herds of domestic horses, all in dude-ranch-type atmospheres. The herds have ranged in number from thirty-five horses to eighty or more. Each herd was pretty stable (no pun intended) from one year to the next. That is, there were few, if any, new horses coming into the herd, and few horses going out of the herd. As a result, there wasn't much jockeying for position within the herd once it was established.

In each case, the herd took on a very similar look to that of Kit's herd. They all started with a small number of boss horses or alphas. From there the herd branched out into a number of smaller satellite bands, each of which was led by a horse that seemed to have been chosen as a leader by the other members of the band.

In each herd, the alphas were clearly not interested in making friends with any of the others and would exert their dominance every chance they got. In fact, I once watched an alpha horse named Scooter single-handedly keep no less than ten horses away from a water tank until he was finished with it. He did this by launching two full-blown attacks on a couple of horses that ventured too close; then he kept the rest at bay with menacing glances. When he left the tank, the horses parted and let him through as if he was Moses at the Red Sea. It was very clear that those horses were afraid of Scooter and what he was capable of doing to them. Some people would say that the horses respected Scooter and his position as an alpha. I guess I saw it a little differently, and I think the horses did, too.

On the other hand, whenever one of the "chosen leaders" or, for lack of a better term, the *passive leader*, from one of the satellite bands came to water, he or she was almost always followed by other members from that particular band. In almost every case, the passive leader would begin to drink while the others stood quietly nearby. Once the leader had taken several swallows from the tank, the others would slowly move in and they would all drink together. There were no threats, no attacks, and no fearful reactions. When the leader left the tank, the others willingly followed.

Watching the horses in these herds interact was an eye-opening experience for me. It was the first time it really dawned on me just what the old man had been talking about when he told me about horses wanting to "conserve energy." It was also becoming clear that horses actually give some thought as to how they choose to conserve that energy throughout the day. Primarily they conserve energy in a herd situation by willingly following a leader that they know won't cause them unnecessary stress or aggravation. In the herds that I had a chance to work with, it was evident that seldom, if ever, was the chosen leader the alpha horse. Rather, it was a horse that had proven its leadership qualities in a quiet and consistent manner from one day to the next. In other words, it was a horse that led by example, not by force.

Now before you get the wrong idea here, please allow me to explain something. I am certainly not trying to pass myself off as some kind of authority on equine herd behavior, because I surely don't consider myself one. I'm just passing along a few observations

I've made of horses within the herd that ended up having a considerable impact on the way I've looked at and worked with horses over the years.

Years ago when I worked with the old man, I noticed he had a way of going that made everything he did seem very comfortable. He, too, led by example, much as the passive leaders within horse herds seem to. He was always considerate and thoughtful with both horses and people and never used force with either unless it was in self-defense. The horses on his place responded very positively to his way of going, and as a result, his horses were consistently willing, responsive, and friendly. Looking back, I guess I just figured that was the way all horse people were. But as I grew older, I came to find that wasn't the case. Many people don't hesitate to exert their dominance over their horses. It's these folks who seem to have horses that are untrusting, unwilling, and sometimes defensive in nature.

As the years have gone by and I've had the opportunity to see and work with more and more horses, I've come to realize that the more quiet consistency I use in my day-to-day work with them, the better response I get. On the other hand, the more inconsistent I am with my horses, the more problems they seem to develop.

Here is a case in point. Years ago I ran a small horse-training school in which we used newly captured mustangs as the subject horses for the classes. The first year of classes, we would start handling and training the mustangs almost as soon as they came to us, which didn't allow them much time to get to know us or for us to get to know them. As a result, the horses seemed to have a hard time understanding and retaining even the simplest of things that we tried to show them during the early stages of their training.

After that first year, we gave the entire situation some thought and came to the conclusion that perhaps the reason our horses had so much trouble was because they were on overload. So much had happened to them during the few months between their capture and the time they arrived that they were completely disoriented— literally. The way of life they'd grown up with was gone, as were all of the horses that they had grown up with. The structure their herd had provided was no longer there, and in its place was a bunch of people trying to tell them what kind of horse they were to become. Their lives had been turned upside-down, and they were having a difficult time coping with just the routine things, much less a regimen of training on top of that.

So, the second year we tried something different. Instead of putting the mustangs directly into the training program when they arrived, we decided to give them a little "decompression" time first. We gave them time to get used to their surroundings without handling them, while making an effort to put some semblance of structure back into their day-to-day activities.

The way we did this was to place the mustangs in separate pens but within eyesight of one another so they at least knew that they weren't alone. We implemented a strict feeding program in which the mustangs were fed at the same time every day. Their pens were cleaned at exactly the same time every day, as well. Our plan was to give the horses something that they could depend on from one day to the next, even if it was just getting their feed or having their pen cleaned. From the day they arrived, they found that when the sun came up over the mountain, someone would be at their pen with hay. When the sun was high in the sky, someone was coming by to clean the pen. When the sun started to go down, someone would come with more hay—all at the same time each day.

During the first week-and-a-half, the mustangs remained very leery and ran to the far end of the pen when someone came around. During the next week or so, they became nervously inquisitive and were less fearful when people came in the pen. By the third week, they were accepting our presence and often had become quiet enough that we could begin working with them. Not all of the mustangs were ready to work after three weeks. Some took longer, some not quite so long. But in every case, once training started, they were in a much better mental state and seemed more able to handle the things we were trying to show them.

The funny thing about all this is that during the first three weeks we did absolutely nothing with the horses that most folks would consider training. And yet those three weeks seemed to make the difference in the horses being able to accept what would happen in the future. In short, I think it showed them that we weren't interested in harming them, and so they were able to let their guards down just a little. At that point, they started seeing us as someone they could possibly put some trust in. The hard part was being able to keep that trust once it was given to us. And the three things we found that helped more than anything else in keeping their trust were to be quiet, consistent, and dependable at all times—much like that passive leader that horses choose to follow when they live in a herd.

When it comes right down to it, I think it's just like the old man said. There's something about horses that we all need to understand—their only real job in this world is to stay alive from one day to the next. Nothing else really matters.

I believe that once we understand that one small, but extremely important, thing about horses—and I mean really understand it—then and only then can we start to bridge the gap between us. After all, that's a bridge that only they can show us how to build. Oh, sure, we may have the tools to build it, but it's the horses that have the blueprint.

NOTES FOR THE NATURE OF THE HERD

Herd dynamics have always fascinated me. As a kid I always wondered why some horses got along so well with others, while other horses couldn't seem to get along at all. It was only as I got older and began to understand that there was actually a rhyme and reason to what the horses did, and how they did it, that it all started to make sense to me. I have come to understand over the years that the most important part of herd structure and dynamics really boil down two things. Keeping balance within the herd and conserving as much energy as possible—both as a group as well as within each individual.

In this chapter I wanted to begin a discussion about how horses see the world they live in. A horse's world is not really one of pushing and shoving and fighting, as some folks might want us to believe. But rather it's one of wanting to get along, whether with other horses in a herd or with the people they come in contact with. From a training standpoint, this can actually make our jobs quite easy because when we work from the standpoint that most horses just want to find a place of solace and comfort, then all we have to do is find a way to create that place for them.

On the other hand, by coming at them with the "alpha" mindset (as it is taught and understood by many trainers and instructors) we are often entering into the situation with the horse's discomfort as our primary goal. A more popular way to say that might be that we are looking for ways to make the wrong thing difficult for them and the right thing easy.

Of course that is not to say that a horse may not become uncomfortable regardless of what we do or how we present the information we are trying to impart. Becoming uncomfortable is part of life, and is even more a part of life when trying to learn something we don't fully understand. However, for my money there is a big difference between trying to make a horse understand something and trying to help a horse understand. Hopefully, by trying to recognize the true nature of herd dynamics, it can begin to help us learn how to bridge that gap.

Otis and Buck

His arrival was rather unceremonious. Standing in the stock rack of an old pickup truck, the elderly sorrel gelding named Otis was thin and in poor condition all the way around. The pickup pulled into the pasture and backed up to the old man's driveway, which was elevated fourteen or so inches above the pasture. Once the bumper touched the rise of the driveway, a heavyset, cigar-chewing man in a sleeveless T-shirt climbed out of the cab and walked to the back of the truck.

The old man was already there and he wasn't making much of the small talk that he usually made when horses were brought in. He looked over in my direction.

"Go grab a halter," he called.

I pulled a halter and lead rope off the large nail just inside the barn door and returned to the old man. He took the halter from my hand and nodded for the heavyset man to lift the gate on the stock rack. The man grabbed a dirty rope attached to a pulley toward the top of the gate and began pulling downward until the gate lifted. Once the gate was about halfway up, the old man ducked his head and climbed into the back of the pickup.

"I know he don't look like much right now," the heavyset man said, with a hint of sadness in his voice, "but he really was a pretty nice horse in his day."

The old man gently approached the gelding and slipped the halter over his nose. He slowly reached over the horse's neck and grabbed the strap of the halter, passing it over the horse's poll and buckling it in place.

"I should've never sold him to them folks in the first place," the man grunted. "He's too good of a horse to have been treated this way."

The old man nodded and motioned for the man to open the gate the rest of the way. With a great deal of squeaking and scraping, the gate was raised and anchored. The old man stood in place until the gate was solid, then slowly led the gelding off the back of the truck. With the exception of a slight hesitation right at the back of the truck, the gelding unloaded without trouble. He stepped over the gap between the truck bumper and the driveway, walked down the drive, and thrust his head into the grass.

The old man allowed him to graze for a short time before gently tugging on the lead rope and bringing the gelding's head up. He turned and led the horse toward the back of the barn where a corral had been cleaned and was waiting. He led Otis through the gate and pulled the halter off. The gelding went straight over to the feed trough brimming with fresh grass hay and began eating.

It would be nearly a month before Otis gained enough weight to be ridden. Even at that he was still a little thin, and since I weighed only about eighty-five pounds, I'd been chosen to take the first ride on him. I quickly learned that the heavyset man had been right about Otis . . . he was definitely a great horse. He was extremely responsive and willing and would go just about anywhere you pointed his nose, including crossing water and bridges, stepping over fallen trees, and side passing to open gates. In fact, he was one of the most responsive horses I'd ever had the pleasure to ride.

Otis continued to be kept in his pen over the next several weeks so he could regain his weight, and the old man told me to make sure he got his daily exercise. Usually I would saddle him up and take him for short rides on the trails through the fields out behind the place. Each day Otis would see me coming, halter in hand, and meet me with a whinny at the gate. He seemed genuinely happy to see me and would leave the pen with exuberance as we headed to the tack room to get saddled up. Once saddled and out on the trail, Otis never refused anything I asked of him. It didn't matter what the task, he would perform it with precision and a willingness I'd never seen in a horse before. In fact, after several weeks of dally rides with Otis, I became convinced that he was simply *the* perfect horse.

Unfortunately, my idea of him being *the* perfect horse began to change one sunny, warm afternoon. On that day the old man decided Otis had recovered enough weight and muscle that he no longer needed to live by himself in a pen. It was time he was introduced to the rest of the herd so that he could be turned out to pasture with them.

The old man had a simple way of doing this. He took Otis from his old pen and placed him in a pen right next to the large pasture that held the rest of the herd. The horses in the herd could all come over and get to know Otis over the fence. In that way, there would be a physical barrier between them that would cut down on the injuries that often occur when a new horse is placed into an established herd. Once the horses got to know one another over the fence, something that usually took a few days, he would turn Otis in with the herd. By that time, Otis would hopefully have learned which horses in the herd to stay away from and which ones might be potential buddies.

I don't mind saying that I was pretty concerned about Otis's well-being when he was turned out in the new pen. All I could think of was this "perfect horse" taking a royal beating from the horses in the herd, even if it was just over the fence. He was such a mild-mannered, kind-hearted guy that I couldn't see how he would be able to defend himself. He just didn't seem to have it in him to be able to protect himself from the attacks that would surely come from the dominant members of the herd, particularly from the one horse that had been the boss of the herd for as long as I could remember—a big, bay gelding named Captain.

I'd already prepared Otis's new home by filling the water tank and placing hay in the feeder close to the gate. As was his custom, he met me with enthusiasm at the gate of his old pen and allowed me to halter him without any trouble. I led him over to his new pen and turned him loose, closed the gate, and stood by to watch what, if anything, would transpire.

Otis went directly to his feed and began eating. Out in the pasture, the herd was clear over in the far corner, and it was several minutes before any of them noticed him. As I expected, Captain was the first to catch a glimpse of him. From a quarter mile away, I could see Captain's head come up out of the tall grass and look over in Otis's direction. His ears were erect and his body suddenly took on a very rigid look.

Otis seemed unfazed and continued munching away at the hay in his feeder. That is, until Captain began making his way over to the corral. About that time, Otis's head popped out of the feeder and he snapped a sudden stare in Captain's direction. Captain went from a slow walk to a trot and finally to an all-out run. The rest of the herd jumped to attention and followed closely behind. All in all, it was quite a sight watching thirty-five horses, led by the big bay, all running hell-bent-for-election toward Otis.

My attention had switched from the herd to Otis, who was standing only a few feet away from me, when something very strange happened—Otis took on a different look from anything I'd seen over the past several weeks. It was almost like watching Clark Kent change into Superman!

Otis went from this quiet, docile, lovable little horse grazing quietly on his hay to a massive-looking, stud-like monster, right before my eyes. I swear, as I stood there watching him, he grew ten inches and changed color! Not only that, but the closer the herd got to him, the bigger Otis seemed to get. As he grew, the muscles rippled under his skin. He stomped his feet like he was mad at the ground, shook his head, and squealed as loudly as I'd ever heard a horse squeal.

Otis suddenly charged and met the other horses just as they reached the fence. By this time Otis's eyes had changed from the soft brown color that I'd become accustomed to, to a blazing, fiery red. There were also bursts of fire and smoke billowing from his ears and nose—rather impressive all the way around.

Otis's electrifying stature was not lost on the other horses and, for the most part, they stopped just short of the fence with a look on their faces that said something like, *We're not sure if we want to get too close here. This guy is making us a little nervous.*

Captain, on the other hand, was not put off in the least and approached Otis without hesitation. By this time Otis was nearly twenty feet tall, and he arched his neck over the fence in a most impressive greeting. Captain also arched his neck, but he only managed to look like one of those wooden horses from the merry-go-round I'd seen at the carnival. The two snorted across the fence for a couple of minutes before Otis reached out and, with his teeth now six inches long, bit Captain soundly on the neck. Captain wheeled and kicked toward Otis with both hind feet. Otis didn't even flinch. Captain kicked again, hitting the fence post with his left hind foot. The post didn't flinch either, and the shock of hitting something solid took Captain by surprise. He trotted off a little ways, limping slightly on his left hind foot, before returning and going nose-to-nose with Otis once more. Otis bit Captain again, this time on the cheek, then on the neck. Captain retreated.

The other horses kept their distance and seemed somewhat bewildered at Captain's inability to faze Otis. After all, Captain had been the boss of the herd forever. They'd never known a horse that he wasn't able to bully into submission in one way or another. However, in the short time it had taken for Captain and Otis to butt heads, it was becoming clear that Captain had met his match.

Captain returned one more time but made sure not to get within reach of Otis's teeth, which by then were at least ten inches long! Otis was squealing, spinning in place, and rearing. Captain also reared, but it wasn't nearly as dramatic. After several minutes of watching these antics, the majority of the herd had apparently seen enough and began splitting off in different directions. That seemed to bother Captain even more than Otis, and he quickly took out after them, circling, biting, and kicking them until they had formed back up into a large band. Once he had the herd all together. Captain drove them to the opposite end of the pasture, as far away from Otis as he could possibly get them.

So much for me being worried about mild-mannered little Otis.

Over the next couple of days I didn't get a chance to see if the herd was spending much time near Otis's pen. However, by the looks of the bite marks on Captain each morning, it was pretty clear that he, at least, had spent time near the fence. After three or four days, the old man decided it was time to take Otis from the pen and turn him in with the herd.

I went to the pen and, as usual, Otis met me at the gate. The herd was down along the fence line by the road, quite a distance from us. I led Otis through the gate and slipped his halter off, assuming he would run down toward the herd, but he didn't. Much to my surprise, he stood right next to me for several seconds before casually dropping his head to the grass.

I stayed with Otis for a short time, stroking his shoulder, before going back through the gate and heading up to the barn where my chores were waiting. I grabbed a wheelbarrow and scoop shovel, headed back to Otis's pen, and began cleaning. I hadn't been there for more than just a few minutes when I heard a tremendous racket. I looked up to see Captain and Otis, circled by the herd and evidently preparing to do battle. Believing something very bad was about to happen, I dropped my shovel and ran for the old man. I found him in the tack room making some lead ropes.

"I think Otis and Captain are going to get in a big fight out here," I told him, slightly out of breath from the run.

The old man nonchalantly looked up and nodded ever so slightly.

"Is that right?" He slowly climbed out of his chair. "Well, let's go have us a look."

He didn't seem to have much of a sense of urgency, but I didn't waste any time getting over to the pasture fence. By the time I reached the gate, the two geldings were in what looked like an all-out war. They were backing into one another, kicking with both hind feet, then swinging around and biting each other with more than just a little ferocity. After a short time Captain ran off a little way, but Otis was close behind. Once Otis caught up with him, the fight resumed, with even more enthusiasm. Within about thirty seconds, however, the whole thing was over.

About then the old man came sauntering up, cigarette between his lips. Captain had already loped off to the far end of the pasture and Otis was circling the herd.

"Looks like ol' Cap's days of ruling the roost may have finally come to an end," he said, as he watched Captain hightail it for the back forty.

"Shouldn't we do something?" I asked, a little concerned.

"There's nothin' *to* be done," he replied. "They've already taken care of it."

With that, the old man turned and went back about his business, and I was left to contemplate the situation. There were two things about what had just transpired that I found astonishing. The first, of course, was the ferocity with which Otis was able to assert himself. I simply couldn't understand how a horse that was so docile and friendly with people could be so "mean" with other horses. The second thing that amazed me was how quickly he was able to take control of the herd from Captain, the horse that had been in charge seemingly forever. The whole thing was a wonderment to me.

Over the next several weeks I watched the dynamics of the herd, and it was both interesting and confusing to me. On one hand, it was clear that Otis had become the boss of the entire herd. On the other hand, there was still a sort of power straggle going on. In fact, within a few days, Captain was able to steal a few horses back from Otis, although, as I recall, Otis didn't really put up much of a fight. It was almost as though he had *allowed* Captain to have the horses. The next time Captain started sneaking a little too close to Otis and his group, however, Otis put on a full-blown attack that sent him scurrying for cover and put a damper on Captain making future attempts at covert reconnaissance missions.

The herd was split into two distinct bands. Otis held the larger band of around twenty-five head, and Captain led the smaller band of about ten head. The two bands seldom came within more than twenty-five yards of each other, but when they did, token fights usually broke out between the two principals. The fights never lasted long and didn't change the overall herd dynamics. In other words, no horses switched bands.

As time went on, I saw that there were definite similarities in the ways Otis and Captain kept control of their respective bands and how the bands, in turn, responded to them. One fact that was evident was that neither Otis nor Captain were afraid to use force when they felt they needed it, and even when they didn't.

One morning I got to work and the air was still rather cool from the night before. The two bands of horses were grazing quietly out in the pasture. As the morning wore on and the temperature

rose, the horses migrated toward the two shade trees along the fence line. Otis and Captain remained out in the middle of the pasture, but the rest of the horses were soon standing quietly under the trees, their tails lazily swishing back and forth.

This lasted only a short while before Otis, and then Captain, began to approach the shade trees. Before they were within thirty feet of the trees, the other horses began to act uneasy. Some cocked an ear in the direction of the boss horses as they approached, then side passed out of the way. Others simply left the comfort of the shade without hesitation. Still others laid their ears back and flicked their tails, but they, too, eventually began a slow retreat. No matter how the horses chose to leave the shade, they had one thing in common—a look of total resignation.

It took less time for the entire herd to evacuate the shady spots than it took for the two boss horses to walk from the middle of the pasture to the trees. Soon Otis was standing alone under one tree and Captain was standing alone under the other. The rest of the horses were back out in the heat of the day. Once in a while, one of the horses from the herd would attempt to sneak back under one of the trees, and each time they were met with a vicious charge from one of the bosses, sending the horse racing back to the relative safety of the herd.

Later that afternoon when the heat dissipated a little, Otis and Captain finally relinquished their grip on the precious shade trees. As they approached the water (where most of the herd had gathered when they were banished from the trees), the horses quickly parted and let them pass, although they sure didn't seem too happy about it. Each horse flicked its tail and laid its ears back as it trotted out of the way. Even at that, Otis attacked at least two horses from behind as they retreated, and Captain attacked one.

Otis and Captain were ruling their respective bands with an iron fist . . . even when an iron fist clearly wasn't needed. Attacks on unsuspecting herd members were frequent and often without provocation. On one occasion I watched in amazement as Otis harassed a young gelding named Rebel. Rebel was resting near the edge of the pasture, and Otis was grazing peacefully some forty feet away. Seemingly without cause, he suddenly lifted his head and charged Rebel. Rebel wheeled and tried to get out of the way, but Otis still caught him on the hip with a nasty bite.

This type of encounter was more the norm than the exception with both Captain and Otis. Each made their share of seemingly unprovoked attacks on herd members, every day, sometimes ending in physical contact, such as a bite or a kick, and sometimes not. There didn't seem to be much rhyme nor reason to the attacks, other than they appeared to be some kind of attempt by the boss horses to reinforce their dominance over the other members of the herd.

If one of the boss horses came near one of the herd members, the herd member was clearly uneasy. For instance, when Otis or Captain approached, the horse would quit grazing and focus on the boss horse. If an attack came, obviously the horse would run off. If an attack didn't come, the horse went back to grazing but with its head turned away from the boss, perhaps in an attempt to look as nonthreatening as possible or perhaps just as a way to save some steps in case an attack did come. As herd members grazed, they almost always headed away from the boss, always keeping an ear cocked in that direction, as if never trusting what the boss horse would do next.

The "lesser" members of the herd understood without a doubt who the bosses of the pasture were, and none seemed too interested in challenging Otis's or Captain's authority. However, I noticed something that I thought was pretty interesting.

You see, the herd members were very peaceful and they seemed to get along with one another quite well. There was never much turmoil amongst them. On the other hand, the attitude of the entire herd changed dramatically whenever Otis or Captain came around. The atmosphere went from one of calm camaraderie and mutual respect to one of strong, palpable uneasiness. I attributed the uneasiness to the fact that the boss horses were not only relatively mean to the rest of the herd, but were also unpredictable.

Up to that point I'd been under the impression that most horses within a herd looked up to the boss horses with a sort of awe or with undying respect. But as I watched the herd react to Otis and Captain, I got a whole different picture of how the horses looked at their leaders. It wasn't with awe or respect at all, but rather with mistrust and, in some cases, downright fear. In fact, the majority of the herd usually did everything they could to avoid *any* contact with the boss horses.

Now to be honest, at the time I never gave these "herd dynamics" all that much thought. I pretty much just took the whole thing at face value and left it at that. It wouldn't be until years later that the true importance of what I had witnessed in that herd finally hit home with me.

———————

There had been some talk going around about this lady who was training horses using a new technique she'd recently learned from a trainer out West. This technique was touted as the most humane horse-training technique to date, because it imitated actual horse behavior. The basic premise was that the trainer would take on the role of the alpha or boss horse during training. Because it was assumed that subordinate horses in a herd responded to the alpha out of trust and respect, training would be easy. All reports I'd heard about the method and the lady were very positive, and as luck would have it, I was able to attend one of her demonstrations on this revolutionary training technique.

As the lady entered the arena and began talking, I couldn't help but like her right off. She seemed kind and friendly and, after a few brief introductory words, gave a short description of what she was going to be doing and how she would do it.

She explained how horse herds were structured, beginning at the top of the pecking order with the alpha and beta horses, or the boss and boss-in-waiting (so to speak). She explained how these two horses basically rule the herd and "teach" the others how to respond correctly to their wishes. They did this by exerting their dominance over a particular horse in the herd until the horse in question submitted.

As an example, she spoke about a situation where a particular horse in the herd had done something that the alpha didn't care for. When this occurred, the alpha, usually a dominant mare, but sometimes a gelding or stallion, would run the horse from the herd and keep it from the herd until the banished horse showed by his or her body language that it had submitted to the alpha's will. This body language would include a licking of the lips, a lowering of the head while the horse moved in a large circle around the herd, an overall softening of the body, and finally, facing the alpha with its head lowered in a submissive posture. She, as the trainer, would be looking for all of these things as she worked with the horse that was standing in the round pen.

With that she turned and entered the round pen, holding only a long whip in her hand. The horse was standing quietly in the pen. It turned to look at her as she walked through the gate, but other than that, it appeared rather uninterested.

"As you can see," the lady said, after latching the gate behind her, "our horse is completely ignoring me and showing me no respect whatsoever."

With that, the woman moved to the center of the round pen. She uncoiled the whip, brought it slowly behind her with her right hand, and then quickly and skillfully brought the whip forward and flicked her wrist. The tail of the whip snaked out within about two feet of the horse's hindquarters and made a very loud CRACK! The horse about jumped out of his skin and immediately began running. The lady once again cracked the whip behind the horse, which sent him running even faster. There was a fearful look on the horse's face as he raced around the pen, but that didn't seem to concern the woman, who continued to snap the end of the whip just shy of the gelding's hindquarters.

"What I am doing," she explained, as the horse flew around the inside of the pen, "is letting this horse know exactly who is boss. He wasn't paying attention to me, so now I'm *making* him pay attention. Basically, I am now acting like the alpha horse of the herd."

Within a short time, between cracks of the whip, the horse began throwing glances in the woman's direction as if asking, *What do you want? What have I done?* But the woman either didn't see the looks or didn't care, because she just kept right on cracking her whip, and the horse kept right on running.

After about twenty minutes, when the horse was near exhaustion, he finally lowered his head enough to please the lady. It was then and only then that she quit cracking the whip. Appearing very obedient and submissive, the horse quickly turned in and faced her. His body was sweaty, he was blowing hard through his nose, and his head was definitely very low.

"There," the woman said, as she coiled up her whip. "Now I have this horse's attention and respect, and you can bet that he sees me as the alpha horse of our little herd, which consists of just him and me. You can see that he is now very content and ready to do whatever I ask of him."

I glanced over at the horse, and suddenly the woman's voice faded as I noticed in him something that I hadn't seen in a horse in quite a while. (Or perhaps I'd seen it, but didn't pay it any mind.) What I saw in the horse wasn't a look of contentment, as the trainer had suggested, but a look of resignation. Sure enough, it was the same look I'd seen in the eyes of the horses that had been under the rule of Otis and Captain all those years ago. It was a sadness that started in the eyes and permeated outward until it consumed the entire body.

About then it dawned on me. This woman had indeed accomplished exactly what she had set out to do. In that horse's eyes, she *had* become the alpha.

His registered name is Alms Setter Bar, but everyone knows him as Buck. He originally came from Minnesota in a trade for a trailer, if memory serves me correctly, and he spent most of the first seven years of his life in one pasture or another and was handled very little. I first learned about him over a few beers at the Wheel Bar in downtown Estes Park, Colorado, with my good friend, Dwight

Thorson. Dwight and I had spent most of that day moving cattle on the ranch he was running at the time. Once the work was done, we stopped at the local watering hole to wash down some of the dust with a cold one . . . or two.

As it almost always happens when Dwight and I get together, the talk eventually turned to horses. As I recall, we began by discussing his draft horses and how well-mannered they were. You see, a few days earlier I had driven out to the ranch while Dwight was plowing in the field with a four-up of Percherons. When he saw me drive in, he asked the team to whoa, draped the lines over the seat, and walked over to my pickup. We talked for only a short time before he mentioned that he needed a cup of coffee. With that, we headed into his workshop just a short walk away. Dwight poured himself a cup, and we sat and visited for the better part of thirty minutes. Once we had gossiped about as much as either one of us could stand, we headed out of the shop. Over in the field his four blacks were standing right where he had left them, lines still draped over the seat. They hadn't moved a muscle as far as I could tell.

As we sat in the Wheel, I couldn't help but mention how impressed I was at how well-behaved his team had been.

"That's how they're supposed to be," he said, nonchalantly. "A runaway draft horse ain't much good to anyone."

Yes, sir. That certainly made sense. At any rate, as the night wore on, Dwight suddenly asked if I'd be interested in taking one of his saddle horses off his hands.

"He's a half brother to my Red horse," he told me. Dwight had raised Red and rode him just about every day. He was one of those horses that made you wish you had about a hundred just like him. He was one great horse and Dwight was extremely proud of him.

"We haven't done much with this guy, and he sure ain't nothin' fancy. He's just standing in the pasture getting fat. He's seven years old. I think he'll be a pretty good horse if someone will just work with him some. Hell, if you want him, you can have him."

"I can have him?" I asked. "What do you mean, I can have him?"

"I'll just give him to you," he shrugged. "I'll never use him. You want him?"

"He's registered?"

"Yup."

"Dang, Dwight. He's a half brother to Red? Are you sure you want to do that?"

"The only thing I'd ask," he motioned for Marlin, the big guy behind the bar, to fill our glasses, "is that you let my dad ride him once in a while when he comes out here from Minnesota. Or let me use him if I need an extra horse or whatever."

"That's it?" I questioned.

"That's it."

"Well," I shrugged, "I guess I can live with that. What's his name?"

"Buck," he said flatly. "I don't know why he's called that, though. I doubt he's got one in him."

And with that, the deal was made.

Dwight had been right on in his description of Buck. At first glance there is nothing at all fancy about him. He's just a red horse with a stocking on his left hind and a small star on his forehead. Even though he was relatively plain to look at, it didn't take me long to find out that Buck was, in reality, no ordinary horse.

Shortly after picking Buck up from Dwight's place, I started working with him. His training went smoothly, and before long, the two of us were out riding the trails. Over the next couple of years I spent part of just about every day either riding or working with Buck in one way or another . . . not so much because I was trying to "train" him, but because I simply enjoyed his company. As a result, he and I went everywhere and did just about everything a horse and rider could do together.

We gathered a herd of about twenty horses from the forest in the middle of the night, after one of my employees accidentally left a gate open. We roped a thousand-pound steer that had jumped a fence, and we acted as outrider for a four-up of Belgian draft horses pulling a wagon during several parades. We volunteered for the local search-and-rescue and brought several injured folks out of the mountains—one we brought down from an elevation of over 11,000 feet in the middle of the night. When the local rodeo queen's horse was injured, she borrowed Buck, and he carried flags the size of large picture windows at a full run in front of 5,000 cheering people at six rodeos. He had never done anything like that before in his life, but he never faltered.

Once, while riding through the mountains, I heard a loud racket behind me. I turned to see my dog, Sadie, being attacked by a coyote. Without thinking, I pulled my .22 rifle from the scabbard, turned, and fired a round over the coyote's head, which was enough to send him running into the hills. The interesting thing was that I had never trained Buck to stand still while someone shot a gun from his back. He just did it for me, no questions asked. Because he stood so well, I was able to save Sadie from being coyote lunch.

Over the years, Buck has taught more people how to ride than either one of us can remember. He's carried everyone from six-year-old children to professional football players and movie actors. One of his most shining moments, however, was when he gave riding lessons to a woman in her mid-thirties who had been a paraplegic since the age of eighteen. When her week of lessons were over and we had helped her back into her wheelchair, Buck, who was standing ground-tied nearby, slowly walked over and put his head quietly in her lap. The woman's husband snapped a picture of the two of them together that I keep in an honored place in our home to this day.

I've never been one for showing horses, but several years back Dwight called me and said that he was taking one of his three-year-old colts to a local horse show "just to get him used to the commotion." He asked if I'd like to go along. I didn't have much else to do that day, so I agreed. Now, as I said, Buck and I had never been to any shows, but because this was more of a "fun day" than a full-blown horse show, we went ahead and entered a few classes. Well, actually, we entered all of them. Twelve in all. The classes ranged from trail classes, barrel races, and jumping courses to tacking up your horse blindfolded. When the dust had settled at the end of the day, Buck and I had placed in the top three in nine out of twelve classes and ended up taking reserve high point, which won us a belt buckle. Unfortunately, the buckle didn't fit Buck, so he gave it to me to wear—which I still do to this day. It's the one and only show either one of us have ever been in.

Now, of all the things we've done together and all that I've learned from Buck during our time together (which in and of itself is immeasurable), nothing compares to the lessons he has taught me about how a true leader should act with his or her peers. Very early on, I noticed something different about how other horses responded to Buck and how he responded to them when he was in a herd.

Shortly after I moved Buck up to a ranch where I had just been hired to run the horse program, the distinction became apparent. After a few days of keeping Buck in a pen next to the large, dry-lot pasture where the ranch's horse herd was, I saw that he wasn't really having any problems with the horses in the herd and decided to turn him in with them. There were about thirty-five head in the pasture at the time, and as soon as I closed the gate, it was obvious that Buck was the "new kid on the block." Every horse in the herd came over to him, sniffing, squealing, and feigning kicks and other threats, but Buck just headed for the feed bunk. With his head buried in the hay, Buck all but ignored them, and most of the herd members soon lost interest in the newcomer and simply went about their business. Pete, the boss of the herd, was not so easily put off, and he continued to badger Buck by pawing at him and throwing kicks in his direction.

After about five minutes, when one of the kicks connected harmlessly to the fatty part of Buck's chest, Buck nonchalantly moved off. Pete chased him, nipping at his hindquarters and lower back legs, forcing Buck into a slow trot as he moved away. Pete followed close behind. Now, the interesting thing was that I had seen Pete do this with other horses in the past. Usually, the horses he chased would take off running for all they were worth with fearful looks on their faces. Buck, on the other hand, didn't look frightened at all. In fact, he appeared more put out by Pete than anything else.

Buck continued his slow trot no matter how much pressure Pete put on him, and suddenly Pete lost interest. Pete broke off the chase in apparent disgust and trudged back over to his favorite feed bunk. On his way to the bunk, Pete laid his ears back against his head as he passed some of the other horses, and they immediately moved out of his way. That was the kind of response he was used to getting from the horses in the herd, and it was apparent that he wasn't very pleased with what had just transpired with Buck.

Buck stayed by himself for several minutes, sort of surveying the herd as they ate. There were six large feed bunks in the pasture, all filled with hay, and all with several horses standing around—except for the feeder where Pete was standing. There were only three horses at that feeder: Pete, B.B., and Cowboy. As I watched Buck look over his options, it was pretty clear that he had decided that the other feeders had way too many horses at them. The practical decision was to pick the feeder with the fewest horses around it. By doing that, he would be more likely to get something to eat. What happened next impressed me so much that it has actually become part of the way I now work with horses.

Buck, having made his decision to eat out of Pete's feed bunk, slowly began to make his way over. He got within twenty-five yards before Pete suddenly wheeled and, with ears flat against his head and teeth bared, charged him. Buck turned and trotted a few paces, which was enough to bring Pete to a stop. He snorted in Buck's direction before shaking his head and returning to the bunk. Buck waited a few minutes, then slowly walked back toward the bunk. Again, Pete pinned his ears and attacked, and again Buck turned and trotted off a few paces. This continued for the next half-hour.

The thing that I found fascinating was that Buck, in a very quiet way, was making Pete's dining experience a totally miserable one. The other item of note was that Buck was doing very little work. During his advance and subsequent retreat, he was only covering an area about fifteen feet in diameter. Pete, on the other hand, was traveling at least fifty feet one way at a dead run each time he tried to run Buck off. In fact, Pete had covered so much ground just trying to keep Buck away from the feed that he had actually broken a sweat.

After that first half hour, a change began to take place. Pete no longer stopped eating to ran after Buck. Instead, as Buck slowly advanced, Pete would abruptly pull his head from the feed bunk, pin his ears, and throw his head up and down as if he were nodding. That caused Buck to freeze in his tracks until Pete went back to eating. When he did, Buck advanced again until Pete eventually pulled his head from the feed bunk, laid his ears back, and threw his head. Buck would stop his advance, Pete would stop throwing his head, and the whole thing would start all over again. By working in this quiet but very persistent manner, Buck had not only worked himself up to Pete's feeder within half an hour but was eating out of it with Pete standing at his side.

I was struck by a couple of things about how Buck handled himself in that situation. First, he was able to accomplish his goal without once relying on any kind of force—even when force was used against him. Second, he remained extremely calm and consistent during the entire process and never used any more energy than what was absolutely needed. While Pete was running fifty feet, Buck was jogging ten. Pete needed to travel another fifty feet just to get back to his feeder, but Buck only had to walk a few feet to get right back where he'd been before Pete came after him. Finally, Pete had wasted so much time and energy that it was easier to let Buck eat with him than continually try to run him off. In the end, Buck sort of won by default.

Several years later I watched as Buck did something very similar when he was put in with a big quarter horse mare that had been on her own most of her life. Now, this mare wasn't on her own because her owner didn't have any other horses to put with her.

She was on her own because she was so mean to other horses. The problem was, I didn't know that.

I was moving Buck to a stall and run for a few days so I could doctor a small cut on his knee. It wasn't a serious cut, but I thought infection could set in if it wasn't tended to. At any rate, the stall wasn't quite ready for him when I arrived at the barn and I didn't want him standing in the trailer while I finished cleaning the stall. The mare was out in a big arena. I'd worked with her in the past and always found her to be easy to get along with. I couldn't imagine that Buck would have any trouble with her if I turned him out for a few minutes while I finished getting his stall ready. So that's what I did. What happened next was one of the most amazing things I believe I've ever seen.

After I turned Buck loose in the pen, the mare came charging up to him in a very aggressive manner. Buck almost completely ignored her. After sniffing him, the mare wheeled and kicked at him, but Buck simply stepped out of the way. The mare reloaded and kicked again, and again Buck stepped out of the way. The kicks never got anywhere near him. It was obvious that the mare was extremely upset, and she turned and tried to bite him. Buck responded by going into the slow trot he had used when Pete chased him. For forty-five minutes, Buck slowly trotted around the arena. He did figure eights, serpentines, and circles, followed closely by the mare the entire time. Because he kept changing direction, even though she was doing everything she could to get her teeth into him, the mare found it next to impossible to get hold of him.

I think it finally dawned on the mare that the longer she tried to be aggressive toward Buck, the harder she was going to have to work. Before long, she slowed her gait, dropped her head, and relaxed her body. When that happened, Buck wandered over and began eating out of a small pile of hay near the gate. The mare followed him closely but didn't try to attack him. Soon they were both quietly eating together.

I left Buck in the arena even after I had finished cleaning his stall and found that, no matter where he went, the mare went with him. If he walked to the water, she followed closely behind. If he stood in the shade, she stood in the shade. About that time, the mare's owner showed up and saw her following Buck around like a puppy dog. She couldn't believe how nice the mare was behaving and told me how her horse usually ate any horse she put her in with and then spit it out. She was astounded. Finally, when I took Buck from the arena, the mare stood at the gate for nearly twenty minutes whinnying for him to return. Buck, on the other hand, quietly stood in his stall and munched away on the hay in his feeder, unconcerned by the entire episode.

Over time, I've noticed many of the horses in whatever herd Buck is a member of seem to look up to him in a way I'm not sure I've seen before. Out of the blue, horses follow him around and, in some cases, even seem to seek him out. He's never run off any horse or acted aggressively toward any horse (even very young ones) that wanted to be near him.

In fact, not long ago, one of our mares foaled unexpectedly out in a pasture with nearly twenty other horses. Somehow the mare and baby became separated a couple of hours after his birth, and the rest of the herd wouldn't let her near him. When we arrived, the baby was standing at Buck's side with the mother nearby. Any time one of the members of the herd tried to get to the baby, Buck would simply go into his slow little trot. The baby would follow, and the horse or horses trying to get at the baby gave up. Because of Buck's help, we were able to get mother and baby safely back together and moved to the barn where they both recovered from the ordeal and went on to do very well.

There are countless times I could mention when Buck has helped "wayward" horses, but there's one situation I find particularly noteworthy. It happened a few years back when Buck was in the pasture with nearly seventy horses. As always, there were a number of horses that followed him around from place to place. A new mare was brought up and turned out in the pasture. The majority of the herd, including the horses that had been following Buck, ran over to investigate the new mare. They circled her, sniffed, squealed, bit, kicked, and finally all ran off, leaving her right where she had been when they approached her.

The mare seemed lost and confused and didn't move from her spot. Buck, one of the few horses that hadn't joined in the "welcoming committee," hadn't moved from his spot either. He was standing some 200 yards away, grazing peacefully. Then, almost as an afterthought, Buck slowly made his way over to the new mare. He stopped nearly fifty yards from her and just stood. He stood quietly for nearly ten minutes before the mare slowly, cautiously approached him. When she finally reached Buck, they sniffed each other for a few seconds before Buck turned and walked back to the place he'd been grazing. The mare, very quietly, followed closely behind. From that time forward, she was accepted into the little band that followed Buck, almost without question.

Since that time I've had the opportunity to observe quite a few horses similar to Buck, who have the same demeanor and effect on horses in herds. Their quiet confidence and lack of force or aggression appears to be something that other horses look for and, when given the opportunity, actively seek out.

It seems to me that if we want to emulate horse behavior during training, we must decide what type of horse we are trying to be like. Should we try to be like Otis and Captain, the boss horses that others seemed to respond to out of fear and distrust? Or do we want to be like Buck, the horse that can find a quiet solution to even the most difficult problems—the leader that other horses *want* to be around and look up to?

The choice is ultimately up to us. But I do have to wonder ... which one would our horses prefer?

NOTES FOR OTIS AND BUCK

I really enjoyed reading this chapter as it brought back fond memories of my horse Buck, who passed away on New Year's Day in 2004. Buck was one of the main reasons this book exists today, as it was his behavior around other horses that really got me to thinking about the concept of the Passive Leader in the first place.

It was Buck that showed me that horses will often avoid unnecessary (and I stress the word unnecessary) movement and conflict and how once the herd structure has been developed, all members usually adhere to the structure without question. They go where the leader goes, stop when the leader stops, drink when the leader drinks, eat when the leader eats, and all is done with very limited stress or anxiety throughout. It was also watching Buck within the herds he was part of that gave me an understanding about the differences between dynamics in domestic herds and feral herds.

In domestic herds, either a gelding or mare will be chosen to take on the role of the leader, as Buck was often chosen in the herds he was in. The sex of the leader just depends on who is exhibiting the qualities the other horses are looking for in a leader.

Also in domestic herds, horses often come and go and so the herd dynamics are frequently in a state of flux. However, that is seldom the case in a feral herd. In the wild, new horses are seldom introduced into an established band unless the stallion brings a new mare into the fold, or a new stallion takes control of the band and ousts the previous stallion. As a result, the herd dynamics are usually very stable and the alpha's role consists mainly of making small disciplinary adjustments—a nip here, a kick there—mostly just to keep order in the band and teach youngsters how to be productive members of the herd.

Domestic herds with horses coming and going will often have a lot more pushing and shoving and biting and kicking than one might see in the wild, simply because the dynamics are changing so frequently. It is for that reason that I think horses that live in domestic herds rely so much on a strong leader they can depend on, whether another horse, or human. If the herd they live in is constantly in more turmoil than is natural, or if the person that works with them is constantly causing more turmoil for them by the way they handle and/or train them, then the horse will actually seek out a leader that will allow them time to decompress and relax, while at the same time offering the guidance they need.

To me, this is the ultimate role of a passive leader. They guide when necessary, and rest when needed. This simple concept helps the horses in the herd stay in balance emotionally, and allows them the stabilization they need to ultimately be able to function properly. Buck was great at this, and it is that same kind of behavior I try to exemplify when I'm working with horses.

Perspectives and Perceptions

During the final days of my senior year in high school, a bunch of us who'd shown interest in attending the local college were invited to visit the campus for a day. It was to be a nice little field trip to show us around and help us decide whether we wanted to attend that institution of higher learning in the fall.

The trip to the campus had been a long time coming, but when the day finally arrived, we all jumped into the waiting bus and bounced our way the twenty-two miles to the campus gates. After leaving the bus and taking the highly structured grand tour for nearly six hours, two things were very clear to me. The first was that a college campus was nothing at all like the campus of a small-town high school with only 1,200 students. The second was that there were an awful lot of kids running around with long hair, hippie beads, and sandals. (It was the early seventies, after all.)

It's been over twenty-five years since I made that trip to the college campus, but I remember one thing that happened during our visit to the art department as though it were yesterday.

We had been marched through each department in relatively short order, without enough time to really see anything or even get a feel for what they did there. I guess it was just to let us know that each department actually existed. At any rate, as we were being rushed through the art department and I was almost out the door, something caught my eye. I just had to stop and get a better look.

Ten or twelve easels stood over by the window. On each easel there was a painting of a tree. I could see the tree that had been used as the model for the paintings. It was a large white oak that stood just outside the window, perhaps fifty yards away. The strange thing was that while each painting looked similar to the others, each was also very different, almost as if every person who had painted one of those pictures had been looking at a different tree.

I had been standing for several seconds, I guess, before a young man with a scraggly beard, long hair, and tie-dyed shirt drifted up.

"We all look at the same tree with different eyes," he said in a sort of mystical way. "It's all perception, man. It's how the individual believes the tree to be. No one is right, and no one is wrong. It's what we do with our perceptions that makes the picture. Cool, huh?"

And with that, he nodded a few times, then drifted slowly away.

I never did attend that college. But the sight of those paintings and what they stood for has never left me. I've never forgotten them because the lesson to be learned from them is so dang important—there is almost always a big difference between what is real and what is perceived.

When it comes to working with horses, I've found this awareness of perception to be especially important. Over the years, I've repeatedly seen that a horse's perception of us and of what we are asking from it can be so far from what we really want or need that trouble is bound to occur from time to time. After all, if ten or twelve people painting the same tree can come up with such varied images, how can we expect our horses to have an accurate perception of everything that we ask of them?

Several years ago when I was teaching the horse-training classes using mustangs, we'd been working with a two-year-old sorrel gelding fresh off the ranges of Nevada. One of the students had named him Elko. The horse had pretty much decided right off the bat that he was going to do whatever it took to get along with whoever was working with him. He was easygoing and picked up the things we were attempting to show him during his training very quickly. The groundwork (i.e., catching, haltering, leading, longeing, ground driving, etc.) took only a couple of weeks. He accepted the saddle without too much fuss, and after only three weeks of handling, seemed ready to accept a rider.

At that point he had already become a master at giving to pressure. He could turn, stop, and back on the long lines softer than just about any horse I had seen. Any time you approached him in an enclosure, he would automatically turn and face you. He would pick up his feet if you simply leaned down toward the foot you wanted, and if you touched his hindquarters or shoulders, he would happily step over without hesitation. At that time, I would have said that his perception and my perception of giving to pressure were exactly the same—when pressure is applied, move away from it instead of lean into it.

It was only when it came time to get into the saddle for the first time that I found our perceptions of how, when, and why a horse should give to pressure weren't at all in sync. Now, before going any further, I should point out that when I get on a horse for the first time, I usually spend a great deal of time getting the horse used to the idea of accepting someone on its back. In other words, I may spend several minutes, hours, or even days putting weight in the stirrups, leaning over the horse's back, moving the leather fenders of the saddle, and the like.

Generally I will continue to do this until I'm fairly certain that the horse is ready to accept a rider in the saddle without incident. Often fifteen or twenty minutes is all it takes. Some horses take much longer, but not the little mustang gelding. It was clear from the start that he wasn't troubled in the least by my routine, as I prepared him to accept me on his back for the first time. So, after spending just a few minutes working with the saddle, I made the decision to climb aboard. I put my foot in the stirrup, bounced a few times, gently swung my leg over, and settled quietly into the saddle.

The little mustang stood for only a few seconds before responding to the weight on his back in the only way that made sense to him. He shifted his weight slowly from one foot to another and took a deep breath. Then, much to my surprise, he lay down.

Looking at it from his perspective, he had been taught that he was supposed to move away from pressure. In that situation, all the pressure—and it was certainly a lot of pressure, at that—was coming from his back. To him, the options seemed limited. His perception of what was expected of him was simple. If he was supposed to give to pressure and there was a lot of pressure on his back, then surely I must have wanted him to lie down. You know what? He was absolutely right to think that way, although at the time it certainly took me unawares.

That episode taught me that the way I perceive horse training and the way my horse perceives that same training may very well be completely different. I felt I needed to start looking at some of the "unwanted" things that my horses were doing during training in a new light. In short, I began to understand that when my horses were having trouble with something I was trying to teach, it didn't automatically mean that they didn't want to perform. In truth, horses almost always want to do the right thing. It's just that sometimes they may perceive the situation differently than I do and, therefore, think that I want something other than what I really want.

I also got to thinking about how I may have misunderstood other behaviors that I'd seen in horses from time to time and that, in the past, I had thought was disrespect or aggression.

A prime example of this sort of misunderstanding was a large, gray gelding named Traveler. Traveler had been raised by his owner, a young woman named Jan. At the time I was asked to look at him, he had just turned four and in the previous year he'd been to three trainers whose sole job was to try to get him started under saddle. It's important to note here that Jan was a very quiet, thoughtful, kind person who was experienced with horses and who had done some very wonderful things with this horse before she'd taken him to the first trainer. She had worked with him so much, in fact, that Traveler was easy to handle, was good with his feet, trailered well, and had even had a saddle on his back a time or two without incident.

Jan told me that she had wanted badly to do the rest of Traveler's training by herself but had just had a baby about the time she was ready to start him. As a result, she didn't feel that she would be able to spend enough time with him to do the job properly. That was why she had taken him to the first trainer over a year before I saw him. Jan had been confident that the training would go smoothly, especially because Traveler had always been so well behaved and willing to learn.

Much to her surprise, only a couple weeks into Traveler's training, the trainer called Jan and told her to pick him up. The trainer went into this long dissertation on how Traveler was a dangerous and very disrespectful horse that was likely to kill someone before it was all over. He told her that Traveler had kicked at him on numerous occasions, had been rearing up, and was even threatening to bite. He went on to say that he wouldn't have such a mean horse on his place and that Traveler must be picked up right away.

Somewhat bewildered by the picture the trainer had painted of her horse, Jan quickly went over with her trailer. She was shocked to find that the trainer's description of Traveler's behavior was actually quite accurate. When she went into his pen to halter him, he quickly spun his butt toward her and threatened to kick. When she finally got the halter on him and began to lead him, he jigged, snorted, and occasionally reared at the end of the line. He balked at the trailer for several minutes before loading and pawed in the trailer all the way home. Once home, Jan found she could no longer approach Traveler without him pinning his ears and baring his teeth in a threatening manner.

Before she'd taken him to the trainer, Jan regularly took Traveler for walks up and down her street in the evenings to give him some exercise and get him used to unfamiliar sights and sounds.

After Traveler came home from the trainer, going for any kind of walk at all, even if it was just from one pen to another, was next to impossible.

With her concerns about Traveler's behavior mounting daily and quickly turning into fear, Jan called another trainer, one known for her quietness in working with horses. The trainer agreed to come and have a look at Traveler to see what, if anything, could be done to help him.

This trainer took one look at Traveler and quickly agreed with the first trainer that he was extremely disrespectful and dangerous. With that, she put him in the round pen and began teaching him some manners. The methods she used, as Jan puts it, were somewhat less than the quiet techniques the woman had become known for. Evidently, there was a lot of whip-cracking, persistent slapping of the horse with a lead rope, and some vicious jerking of the halter. At one point the trainer offered to lay Traveler down in order to let him know who was boss, but Jan refused to let her.

Traveler was pretty submissive after about two hours' worth of the trainer's work. She showed Jan how to use her techniques— techniques that were much more aggressive than Jan was comfortable using. But Jan figured if that was the only way to get Traveler to respond, she didn't have much of a choice. Besides, the trainer assured her that once Traveler understood that Jan was the boss, he would quit trying to exert his dominance over her or anyone else.

Well, in short, it simply didn't work. Instead of Traveler getting better, his behavior became increasingly worse. By that time, Jan was getting to the point where she was so frightened of Traveler that she refused to go into his pen, even to clean it. She was miserable at the thought of not even being able to pet the horse that she could once lead around with nothing more than a piece of baling twine around his neck.

Jan called another trainer who had no luck trying to improve Traveler's attitude and who quickly recommended sending him to the killers before he hurt someone. Heartbroken and at the end of her rope, Jan brought Traveler to a horsemanship class I was teaching in her area. Before bringing him to the round pen, she went into the long explanation of Traveler's background and training experiences, and then, holding back tears, she told me that I was probably Traveler's last chance. If I couldn't help him, she was going to put him down before he killed either her or someone else.

Now, as Jan was recounting all the bad behaviors Traveler had developed over the previous year and how dangerous and disrespectful he'd become, one thing kept sticking out in my mind. Even though he behaved as though he was mean and dangerous, he'd never actually hurt anybody. In each case, when he could have or should have hurt someone with his behavior, even when the trainers were doing some pretty aggressive things to him, he never once kicked, bit, struck, or ran over anyone. He had threatened on several occasions but never actually followed through. That got me to wondering if his behavior was, in fact, stemming from disrespect. Perhaps it was something else entirely.

Traveler was led to the round pen by a very large man whose help Jan had enlisted. I followed the two into the pen and asked the man to turn Traveler loose and leave the pen.

"You want me to turn him loose?" he asked, with a surprised look on his face.

"If you would," I nodded, as I swung the gate shut behind me.

"Okay," he said, with uncertainty in his voice.

He reached up, unbuckled the halter from Traveler's head, and slipped it over the gelding's nose. Traveler responded by wheeling away from the man, running off about fifteen feet, and kicking up with both hind feet before heading to the rail and taking off at a dead ran. The man quickly slipped through the gate and latched it behind him, leaving us alone in the pen.

I moved to the middle of the pen and stood quietly as I watched the gelding make lap after lap, running just as fast as his feet would carry him. Every once in a while he would snort and throw a half-hearted kick in my direction. He had no real chance of coming close to kicking me with the distance that was between us, so for the most part I simply ignored his feints.

"See," I heard Jan say from her spot outside the pen. "See how dangerous he is?"

Now, I guess this is where a little different perspective on what was happening was helpful. Up to that point, Traveler had thrown six or seven kicks, including one in the direction of the fellow who had brought him into the pen. However, Traveler was never close to anybody when he threw a kick. In fact, in the case of the man who brought him into the pen, he was actually running away from him, consciously putting a safe distance between them before kicking.

I began to wonder why, if this horse was truly mean or dangerous, he hadn't simply wheeled and kicked the man with both hind feet, then turned and stomped him into the dirt? For that matter, why wasn't he charging me and trying to stomp me into the dirt, as well? If he was dangerous and disrespectful, why was he running away from me? After all, it seems to me that when a horse is running away from something, he's using his flight instinct, not his fight instinct. Doesn't that mean he's fearful of whatever it is he's running from?

I continued to watch Traveler as he sped around the pen. And, while he was laying his ears back and throwing the occasional half-hearted kick, he certainly wasn't trying to hurt anyone. In fact, it seemed less and less as though he was being disrespectful of me, and more and more like he was trying to protect himself. Traveler looked like a horse in a herd does when it is being moved or pushed around by a more dominant member of the herd.

When a dominant member of a herd moves a less dominant member from a pile of hay, for instance, the dominant horse may chase or even attack the less dominant horse. The less dominant horse, in return, will usually pin its ears and throw a kick in the direction of the horse that's doing the chasing. Seldom will the less dominant horse actually "pull the trigger," if you will, and connect with a kick. It's usually just a hollow warning that tells the dominant horse that although the less dominant horse is leaving, it isn't leaving happily.

That was the look I was getting from Traveler. It was a look of hollow self-defense—a series of unhappy warnings—rather than a look of aggression.

If I was correct in my assumption that he was trying to defend himself rather than pick a fight, it seemed to me that Traveler would want to find some help for himself before too long. He would want to find a way out of the situation without causing himself, or me, any more undue hardship. I decided that I must appear as non-threatening to him as I possibly could. If I was quiet enough for Traveler to put some trust in, maybe he would start looking to me for help.

I continued to stand pretty much in one spot in the middle of the pen with the halter and lead rope draped over my forearm. As he ran, I watched. He made lap after lap, and finally settled into a relatively comfortable trot. After three or four laps in the trot, it became apparent that he was falling into a rhythm that I didn't necessarily want him to get into. Over time, when a horse is in a somewhat stressful situation, they can turn that trotting rhythm into an almost trancelike state of mind. Once in that state, a horse can travel non-stop for a long time with very little effort, which I certainly didn't want in our situation. I needed Traveler's attention on what was going on in the pen so that I could try to help him find a quiet solution to the problem he was having.

For that reason, after he'd made a couple more laps, I quietly made my way toward the rail so that I put myself in his path as he came around. Seeing me, he slammed on the brakes, flipped around, and headed back in the other direction just as fast as he could go—another sign that he wasn't interested in being aggressive toward me.

After Traveler headed the other way, I wandered back to the middle of the pen and waited for him to make the next move. He made several more nervous laps before he suddenly began giving me some very quick glances. With each glance, I shifted my weight backwards, away from him. This offer to remove a little of the pressure he was feeling seemed to be just the thing he needed. Almost as if someone had flipped a switch, he began turning his head in my direction and throwing these long, worried looks at me. I shifted away from him each time he looked at me; and each time I shifted my weight, his looks became longer and more inquisitive.

After a few short minutes, he abruptly turned off the rail and trotted toward me with a worried look in his eyes. I wanted to let him come but was just a little concerned about the speed at which he was approaching. To ask him to slow down a little, I raised my arms slightly at my sides. This little movement surprised Traveler, and he once again slammed on the brakes and backed up several steps, but continued to face me. He was breathing hard and sweating from all the running he'd just done, but he stood perfectly still, as if asking for further instructions.

It seemed clear that he was looking for a little reassurance, and so I slowly made my way up to him and, as gently as I could, stroked him between the eyes. With that his head dropped, his eyes softened, and he let out a long, quiet sigh. I stood petting him for a moment before stepping back to my spot in the middle of the pen. He quietly followed. From that point forward, he would not leave my side. Wherever I went, he went. Whatever speed I traveled, he was right there with me. He wanted badly to be near me but never bumped into me or leaned on me. He stopped when I stopped and moved when I moved. All in all, he was trying as hard as he could to do whatever I asked, even though the things that were being asked of him were extremely small. It was clear that he didn't want to make a mistake, but more than that, it seemed as though he was trying very hard *not* to make me mad.

Over the next several minutes, I tried to reassure him that everything was okay by petting him on his head, shoulders, and back, and he responded by becoming calmer with each passing minute. After a while it was evident that he had become pretty comfortable with me and what I was doing. I figured that was as good a time as any to leave him by himself for a few minutes to think about what had happened and allow things to sink in just a little. With that in mind, I petted him once more between his eyes and left the pen. He followed me to the gate and watched as I slipped out. I must say that what happened next surprised me, mostly because I had never experienced anything like it in all the time that I'd been working with horses.

I had just latched the gate behind me when Traveler let out a soft, low nicker. He was still watching me as I turned and walked over to where Jan and some other folks were sitting. He continued to nicker and mirrored every step that I took with steps of his own inside the pen. If I stopped, he stopped. If I walked, he walked. Each time he stopped, he raised his head over the round pen fence and looked directly at me, nickering the entire time. I walked the whole way around the outside of the pen, and he never once let me out of his sight. He met me at the gate, and as I went back in with him, he acted as though I was his long-lost best buddy whom he hadn't seen in twenty years.

The turnaround in his behavior was so profound that it astonished everyone, including me. He followed me for another lap or two inside the pen before I slowly reached up and offered to slip the halter over his nose. As if on cue, he willingly dropped his nose down into the halter and stood quietly as I buckled it in place. I turned and led him around inside the pen while he followed quietly behind.

I asked Jan if she'd like to come in and lead him around a little (something she hadn't done in nearly three months). With reservation in her voice, she reluctantly agreed. When she entered the pen, Traveler casually looked up at her but was otherwise uninterested. Jan didn't believe that the now extremely quiet Traveler would respond to her as he had to me, and she asked if I would stay with her as she led him around the pen. I happily agreed. As I handed her the lead rope, she looked as though I was handing her a rope with a 900-pound Bengal tiger on the other end and asking her to walk him through the meat section of the local Piggly Wiggly.

The three of us made several tentative laps around the pen, but it was clear that Traveler wasn't the least bit interested in acting up. It didn't take Jan too awful long to realize that Traveler was trying very hard to be a good boy and, as time passed, it was easy to see her confidence in him building. At that point, I moved to the center of the pen and let her and Traveler walk together, alone. The lead line remained loose, Jan's gait was relaxed, and Traveler held his head low and quiet.

Over the next couple of days, Traveler began to regain the trust in Jan that he had lost, just as she was regaining her trust in him. During those days we taught Traveler how to longe and ground drive and had even saddled him a time or two without so much as a blink from him. By the third day, Jan and Traveler were walking all over the ranch together, just as they'd done before she'd taken him to the trainer who had deemed him dangerous and disrespectful over a year before.

Now, I have no idea what happened between Traveler and the first trainer he went to. Perhaps there was some kind of misunderstanding between the two of them that forced Traveler into a defensive mode and frightened the trainer. It's hard to say. One thing I do know for sure is that everybody involved had a different perspective of the situation.

By the time I was asked to work with him, Jan had been convinced by three different professional trainers that her horse was disrespectful and dangerous (even though he had never actually hurt anybody). She had been told that the only way to handle him was with a heavy hand, so he would learn respect and manners. As a result, Jan believed that she had a mean, disrespectful horse that needed to be taught who was boss every time she came in contact with him. Unfortunately, not only did treating Traveler that way not help the situation, it actually made things much worse. With Jan escalating the frequency and intensity of the corrections she gave him, Traveler became so unmanageable that she was afraid to go into the same pen with him.

Traveler's perspective was simpler. Every time a person came near him, his halter was jerked, he was slapped with a lead rope, yelled at, and treated badly in general. As far as he was concerned, he needed to defend himself any time someone on two legs came around. If that scared the people who were jerking and slapping him, so be it. After all, his options were pretty limited. Like the mustang that had been taught to give to pressure and lay down the first time pressure was applied to his back, Traveler was simply responding to the situation in the only way he knew how.

Jan and Traveler had two different perspectives on the same situation, and they were perspectives at opposite ends of the spectrum. You can't get any further away than that.

If Traveler was as upset with everyone around him as he appeared to be, why didn't it take a whole lot more effort on my part to draw out his desire to become quiet and trusting? The truth is, I didn't have to do very much because there wasn't really a lot that needed to be done. You see, when a horse is fearful or in trouble, they almost always start looking for someone or something to help them.

I think it's important to remember that the reason Traveler, or any other horse for that matter, would look for help in a threatening situation is because horses are herd animals. They are highly dependent on other individuals to ensure their survival. You will seldom see a horse all by itself in the wild, because a lone horse in the wild is usually a dead horse. So, from a horse's perspective, there is always safety in numbers, and that is the one thing that every horse knows. The key, then, is to find a way to get horses to see you as the individual who can help them when they need it.

Several years ago a friend asked me to help gather his herd of about 100 head of horses off a 2,500-acre pasture in the foothills of Colorado. The horses were split up into several different bands and were spread out all over the rough terrain of the pasture. The six riders doing the gather were split into two groups of three, and I was in the group that was to cover the south end of the pasture.

At this particular outfit, the home place and its large catch pen are on one side of a busy highway and the pasture is on the other. The pasture and catch pen are connected by a tunnel that passes under the highway, which we passed through to begin our search for the horses. Once the horses were gathered, we would have to drive them out of the foothills and back through the tunnel into the catch pen. If luck was on our side, the gather wouldn't take more than three or four hours.

After about thirty minutes of riding, we came to an old game trail that led us up into the hills and back into the canyons and draws where we hoped to find the horses grazing on the fresh spring grass. We traveled along the trail for the better part of an hour before coming to a ridge overlooking a large draw at the southernmost end of the pasture. Down below us were nearly fifty head of horses grazing quietly. The horses were in a number of small bands scattered all up and down the draw . . . four or five here, six or seven there, two or three up on the side of the hill. The fact that they were all so spread out was likely to pose a problem for us from a gathering standpoint. We decided to give the situation a little thought so that we didn't scatter them even more when we tried to gather them, making our day longer than it needed to be.

We sat quietly on the ridge for several minutes discussing the best way to gather the band together before driving them north to the tunnel and ultimately to the catch pen. As luck would have it, one of the horses down in the draw spotted us up on the ridge and, not exactly sure of what we were, let out a very loud warning snort. It echoed up the draw and quickly alerted the rest of the horses. In less than twenty seconds, all the small bands up and down the draw instinctively grouped themselves together into one large band and nervously milled around in the middle of the draw.

Once the horses banded themselves together, our job looked easy. We simply needed to ease our way down into the draw and quietly push them north toward the tunnel. Well, no sooner had we begun making our way down into the draw than the herd suddenly wheeled and took off running. We scrambled the rest of the way down the trail just in time to see the last horse in the herd head up another game trail that led north, back up the ridge. We moved our horses into a lope across the draw and turned up the trail in pursuit.

By the time we reached the ridge, the horses were already nearly a half-mile away and running hard. We followed as fast as we could, considering the terrain, and finally caught up with them several minutes later in a large valley near the top of the pasture. Much to our surprise, the original herd of about fifty had grown quite a bit. Now there were sixty or seventy horses in the herd, with more horses joining them by the minute. Evidently, other horses that were grazing in the vicinity of the herd, either as it raced past them or as it reached the valley, became alarmed. Instead of assuming there was something dangerous following the herd and running in a different direction for safety, instinct told these horses to join the larger group.

Horses were appearing out of the woods and nearby draws, running as fast as they could and screaming at the top of their lungs. As these horses entered the herd, it looked as if someone had thrown a pebble into a pond. They sent ripples of horses in every direction, permeating outward from the center. There was an awful lot of confusion in the herd itself, which was continually circling without actually going anywhere.

And then something very interesting happened. Looking for an outlet that would lead us to the flat, I rode my horse down into the valley. Suddenly several horses from within the herd began moving toward me. They weren't running or panicked but, rather, seemed to be looking for some help. Once in the valley, I found what looked like the easiest way back down toward the tunnel, and so I rode down the trail a little ways to make sure. After traveling less than 200 yards, I turned around and saw nearly the entire herd following me down the trail. A little surprised, but certainly not willing to look a gift horse in the mouth (no pun intended), I simply turned back around and, followed closely by my two companions who gathered the stragglers, led the herd down the trail and back out to the flat part of the pasture.

I would love to sit here and tell you that the horses saw me riding through the valley and decided that I would make a great leader, which was why they chose to follow me, but I expect I didn't really have a whole lot to do with it. More than likely, the horses, most of which were excited and a little frightened, were looking for a leader to show them what to do next. All of the horses were in a slight state of confusion as to how to get themselves out of the valley. About that time, I rode into the valley on a very quiet horse that appeared to have some purpose in his walk, which he did, due to the fact that we were looking for something specific. I believe some of the horses in the herd saw my horse, figured that he knew where he was going, and decided to follow. After all, he looked quiet and confident and, in fact, did ultimately show them the way out of the valley.

During stressful situations, I believe many horses would rather look to another horse instead of looking to their own riders, particularly if a rider has been less than dependable for the horse in the past. Seems like as far as a horse is concerned, even a strange horse is likely to be trustworthy; if nothing else, at least it will act like a horse. People, on the other hand, sometimes have a little trouble being consistent in their behavior from one day to the next. Because of that, a horse may have trouble trusting our judgment when it really counts.

———————

Not long ago I saw two separate incidents that really drove this point home. In one incident, I was giving a riding lesson in an arena during one of those horse expo things. The horse and rider I was working with weren't the problem. In fact, they were working very well together. It was what was happening outside the arena that caught my attention.

A woman brought over an unsaddled bay gelding and was standing near the gate. The horse was obviously a little worried, what with being in a new place with a lot of activity, people, and strange horses. Every once in a while he whinnied while looking back in the direction of the barn, but otherwise he seemed to be trying to keep himself under control. Just then a gust of wind came up and blew a nearby banner, which flapped loudly right beside the gelding. He jumped several steps away from the banner, jerking on the lead rope the woman held. The woman braced herself, grabbed the rope with both hands, and yelled "whoa" several times at the top of her lungs. This frightened the horse even more, and he backed a little faster. That made the woman yell even louder, which caused the horse to back even faster.

Well, you know that when something like this starts happening it's bound to come to a head sooner rather than later, and that certainly was the case here. By this time the horse was backing so fast that he covered the ground from the gate to the bleachers in pretty short order. Before you knew it, the woman had successfully backed him right smack into the uprights on the side of the bleachers. As you can imagine, that took the gelding by surprise and he jumped forward and almost landed square in his owner's lap.

His owner, although she'd been pulling him forward to prevent his going backward, certainly wasn't ready for that, and so she decided to reprimand him for his "disrespectful" behavior by slapping him several times with the end of the lead rope. That caused the horse to circle around her, which wasn't what she was looking for either, and so she started to jerk on the lead rope to get him to stop circling. Well, the gelding must have figured that this meant he was supposed to start backing again, which he did, which caused the owner to grab the lead rope with both hands and yell "whoa." Of course, the whole thing started all over again, but you get the idea.

From that point forward, the horse could not get himself settled down, and the owner continued to jerk, slap, and yell at him, expecting those things to do the trick. They only made things worse, which made the owner more and more angry, which made the horse more and more upset. Shortly after that, I guess the woman decided that her horse was causing too much of a scene and she took him back to the barn. All the way there, she jerked and slapped, and he jumped forward and circled around her, only to be jerked and slapped some more.

The woman's perception of what was going on was that her horse was being disrespectful because he wasn't responding to her demands. The horse's perspective was that his handler was scaring him, which made him want to get as far away from her as possible.

In contrast, during a clinic I had done a few months before, a fellow had just taken his colt out of the round pen and was leading him back to the trailer to unsaddle him. Over the previous few days, we'd been working on trying to gain the colt's trust, which I felt we had been relatively successful in doing. It was the colt's first time away from home, only the second or third time he'd had a saddle on his back, and the first time he'd carried a rider—all of which he had accepted pretty easily. One of the reasons for this, I believe, was that during the time we were working with him, he had remained quiet and always let us know when he was having trouble with something we were trying to show him. When that happened, we would simply back up a little and work with him until he was comfortable with that task before going any further.

It was the last day of the clinic and he was the last horse we worked before lunch. On the way toward the trailer, the gelding's owner stopped just short of the gate that led out to the parking lot to visit with some folks who had gathered there. All in all, there were probably fifteen or twenty people standing around them or close by.

Suddenly a gust of wind came up and lifted the tablecloth on a nearby registration table. That frightened the colt, and he jumped forward and began running in a semi-panic around his owner. Everyone around the pair scattered, moving very quickly away from the horse. From where I was standing, nearly fifty yards away, I had a very clear view of everything that was happening. I was struck by the fact that there was an awful lot of movement going on over there. People were scrambling in every direction, the horse was running, his mane and tail were whipping in the wind, stirrups on the saddle were banging on his sides, the tablecloth was flapping . . . everything seemed to be in motion. Everything, that is, except the horse's owner.

In amongst all this turmoil was the man who had been leading him over to the trailer, standing quietly and holding on to the horse's lead rope as the horse circled around him. He stood very calmly facing the horse and just letting him circle. The horse made several furious laps around him, then began turning his head from one side to the other, as if looking for some help. Everywhere around him things and people were in motion . . . everywhere except right there at the end of his own lead rope.

I would say that less than fifteen seconds had passed before the colt quieted himself down and trotted up to his owner, who simply reached up and petted him on the head. Even with the tablecloth still flapping in the wind and people running in every direction, the colt had found his help. When the dust settled, people began to return to the pair, more tentatively this time, and continued their conversation. The colt stood quietly at his owner's side and didn't offer to move until the conversation was over and the man turned and led him over to the trailer.

The owner's perception of what was going on was that his horse had become frightened, and he didn't want to add to that fear by reacting in a negative manner toward him. The horse's perspective was that he had become frightened, and he was going to look to the only thing (person, horse, whatever) that showed signs of being able to help him calm his fear.

This horse's owner had just proved to the colt that his judgment could be trusted. It was vastly different from the woman whose horse became frightened and was slapped around because of it.

When it comes right down to it, the whole point of what I am trying to pass along here is that one of the most important parts of horse training really has nothing to do with training at all. It has to do with being able to look at, and understand, the possibility that our horses just may have a different perspective on life than we do. Just because they behave in a way that we don't particularly care for or that frightens us at times, it doesn't necessarily mean that they're being mean or disrespectful. I think we are too willing to look at unwanted behavior from our horses as a sign of disrespect from them. The truth of the matter is, they are almost always acting in a way that they believe to be right, whether they are using defensive behavior, aggressive behavior, or even quiet behavior. The unwanted behavior that we see is usually something that they've been taught, albeit inadvertently, by the people who handle them—like being pushy when being led or pulling back when standing tied. We need to understand that these are learned behaviors, not inherent behaviors.

The thing to remember is that horses are, by nature, very cooperative and social animals. They have to be. It's the essence of living in a herd. The only reason they've survived fifty-million years (without human intervention, by the way) is because they have learned how to get along with and depend on one another.

For the most part, I believe horses want to get along with us and depend on us, too. It's just that we aren't always dependable for them, and so when they get in trouble or when something bothers them, they sometimes search for help somewhere else.

I truly believe that if we can look at the things that our horses do or that we do with our horses with just a little different perspective, it will allow us to find ways to get along with them that don't always initially mean having to exert dominance over them. That opens the door for them to begin to see us as a true leader . . . someone who can be depended upon to make the right decisions for them most of the time. If we can do that for our horses most of the time, they'll forgive us the rest.

(Now, I must also say that, while I do believe this to be true, when it gets right down to it, it's just one person's perspective.)

NOTES FOR PERSPECTIVES AND PERCEPTIONS

While writing this chapter originally, I recall wondering if what I was trying to share was actually going to come across to the reader. You see, when it comes to perspectives and perceptions, the way we humans see things is always filtered by our past experiences and what we believe, what we've been taught or what we've picked up from others. As a result, the filter we see things through often has a tendency to temper reality.

Horses, on the other hand, see everything as it is and take it that way without a filter to run it through first. The bottom line for a horse is, the things around them or that happen to them are either okay and won't potentially harm them, or they will. There is very little middle ground.

If we are presenting information in a way that a horse perceives will harm him, the chances of him willingly going along with what we are offering, or him even trying to figure it out for that matter, go down considerably. If, on the other hand, we are able to offer information in a way that makes sense to him and in which he believes will benefit him in some way, it will almost always be easier for him to look at what we are offering in a little more favorable light, even if what we are trying to teach is difficult for him to learn or comprehend.

I believe understanding this one disparity in our respective perceptions can make the all the difference in the world between ultimately being able to get along with a horse or not. It also a big part of whether or not our horse looks at us as one they can follow, or one he should stay away from.

Finding the Try

"Dang you," I muttered under my breath. "What the heck's your problem?"

It had been nearly forty-five minutes since I'd mounted up, and things were not going well. I was on a young mare named Lacey, and we were working quietly in the round pen when I got the notion to teach the mare how to back up. I started by asking her to stop from a walk, which she did readily. Then I did what everyone knows they're supposed to do when backing a horse—I pulled on the reins. At first, I used what I considered to be pretty light pressure, but she didn't back. I applied a little more pressure. Still nothing.

Several minutes had passed and I continued to increase the pressure until I was not only pulling with my hands, but was also leaning backward in order to get more leverage. If I had to guess, I'd say I was applying just under my total body weight—all seventy pounds of it—to the bit, and she was applying just under seventy-one pounds of pressure back.

This had gone on for quite some time before I started to get tired and my hands began to hurt. I finally had to give in and release the pressure. I laid the reins over the saddle horn and looked at the creases in both hands that the reins had caused.

"Dang," I said, as I began rubbing my hands together to smooth out the creases. "You are one hard-mouthed son-of-a- ..."

"How's it going?" I suddenly heard the old man say from behind me.

Startled, I quickly stopped rubbing my hands together, picked up the reins, and turned the mare in his direction.

"Fine," I blurted. "It's going good."

"How's she working for you?"

"No problems," I said, as I forced a smile and reached down to pet the mare on the neck.

"I see," he nodded. "Whatcha working on?"

"Working on?" I caught myself unconsciously rubbing my hands together, trying to get rid of the ever-growing burning sensation in my palms. "Oh, we're just ... I thought I'd try and ..."

"Get her to stand still?"

"Huh?"

"Stand still," he said, as he lifted his foot and propped it on the bottom rail. "I noticed that the two of you have been standing in one spot for quite a while. Are you working on getting her to stand still?"

"Well, yeah. I guess. Kind of."

The old man slowly nodded his head and seemed to be thinking about something. He ran his hand slowly across his chin and finally leaned both elbows on the top rail of the round pen.

"I believe she's got it," he said, with a slow nod of his head.

"Huh?"

"Standing still." He pointed nonchalantly at the mare. "I believe she's standing pretty well."

"Oh, yeah," I agreed knowingly. "She's doing that pretty well now."

"Probably should think about working on something else then," he said. "Seeing as how she's standing so well for you and all."

"Yeah," I nodded. "I guess I'll work on some transitions."

"You could do that, I suppose." He ran his hand across his chin again. "But what would be even better is if you worked on getting her to back up."

"Back up?"

"Yeah," he nodded. "We should probably make sure she can back up before working on her transitions."

"I don't know." I felt myself wince at the idea. "I'm not so sure that she's the backing-up type."

"Really?" A slight smile crossed his weathered face. "Well, I guess we'll never know until we try, will we?"

"Well, I've kind of tried, but she didn't seem like she liked it very much."

"I see," he nodded again. "How about we give it another go anyway?"

"Okay," I agreed, with a slight ring of sarcasm in my voice. "But I don't think she likes it very much."

With that, I rubbed my hands together one last time, picked up the reins, and slowly began applying pressure to the bit. I could feel Lacey begin to lean on me as her nose jutted forward. I held the pressure for a few more seconds before the creases that the reins had made earlier began to hurt again. With that, I released the pressure and looked over at the old man.

"See," I said. "I don't think she likes it too much."

The old man slowly nodded and walked around to the other side of the round pen. He opened the gate and walked through, quietly closing it behind him. He approached us, petted Lacey gently on the neck, and asked that I try again. I agreed, even though I made it pretty clear that I wasn't too enthusiastic about it.

Once again I reached down and applied pressure to the bit, and once again Lacey began leaning on me by jutting her nose forward.

"Okay," the old man said. "I think I see what the problem is."

Good. He was finally seeing what I had been trying to tell him all along. The dang horse didn't want to back up. It was about time and, frankly, I was a little surprised that it had taken him so long to figure it out. He usually wasn't that slow on the uptake.

"Would you mind if I give it a try?" he asked.

"No," I told him, surprised. "I wouldn't mind at all."

With that, I dropped the reins and began to climb out of the saddle, but he told me to stay mounted. I settled back in the seat of the saddle and put my hands on my waist as he stood next to Lacey and gently picked up the reins. He began to slowly take the slack from the reins but stopped suddenly and gave a little slack back. He waited a couple of seconds and once again began to take the slack from the reins. Again he stopped suddenly, releasing the little pressure he was applying to the bit. He did that three more times

112

when, on the fourth try, I suddenly felt a shift of Lacey's weight backward. The old man released and reapplied the pressure once more, and Lacey gently tucked her nose and drifted ever-so-quietly backward. First one step, then a second, then a third—all in very soft succession.

The old man relaxed his hands and Lacey stopped backing. He set the reins down and quietly stroked the mare on her neck. He waited a few minutes before once again picking up the reins and applying light pressure to the bit. The mare hesitated for a few seconds, and just as I started to believe the first few steps backward were a fluke, she began backing again. This time her steps were a little quicker and even softer.

After she backed for about six or seven feet, the old man set the reins down and stroked Lacey on her neck.

"I guess she doesn't mind backing so much after all," he said. "Why don't you try working on it a little more with her? Just try not to pull so hard and remember that you aren't backing her with the bit. The bit's just there so she can feel the cue." And with that, he turned and walked out of the pen, leaving me to contemplate what had just occurred.

As I watched him disappear around the barn, his words echoed in my ears. What did he mean that I wasn't supposed to back her with the bit? That didn't make sense. Of course I was backing her with the bit. That's what it was there for. Wasn't it?

I took a few more laps around the pen with the mare but never did ask her to back again. The old man's statement had thrown me for a loop, and I didn't know exactly what he meant. His statement sort of paralyzed me; it kept me from wanting to try.

Later, after I finished my ride and put Lacey out to pasture for the day, I went into the barn and started nailing up new boards in the big box stall attached to the tack room. Over the last few days, I'd been working on replacing boards that had rotted over the years and felt I'd be able to get the project finished that day, if the old man didn't find something else for me to do in the meantime.

I don't think I had gotten more than two or three nails driven when the old man appeared in the doorway. He stood quietly in the same spot for several seconds, sort of surveying my work, before reaching in his pocket and pulling out his cigarettes. I drove another nail or two in the board before it finally dawned on me that perhaps he wasn't just standing there in awe of my superior carpentry skills. I got the feeling that he was simply making himself available to answer the question that was on my mind, the one about not using the bit to back Lacey.

"How's it going?" he asked, after lighting his cigarette.

"It's going good," I told him, driving the last nail in the board.

I looked up at him as I turned, set my hammer down, and picked up another board, but I didn't say anything. I wrestled the next board into place. Of course, it was about that time that I noticed I'd forgotten to pick up my hammer and nails. There was no way the board would stay in place if I let go of it to reach my tools, which were a good six feet away. I had no alternative but to set the board back down.

Not wanting to look like a complete idiot in front of the old man for forgetting my tools, I took a very hard look at the board as if making absolutely sure that it fit in the spot I'd chosen for it. Only after sufficient time had passed to make it look as though I was completely satisfied that the board (which had been pre-cut specifically for that spot) fit properly did I finally wrench the board back out of position and set it on the floor. As if it had been the plan all along, I went over and grabbed my hammer and a handful of nails. I put the nails in my mouth, just like all the *real* carpenters do, and stuck the hammer in my belt. Then I wrestled the board back in place and began hammering.

The old man didn't move from his spot. He simply stood, as if watching me hammer nails was the single most important thing he had to do all day. Well, it didn't take long before I had finished hanging the board, and by now it was clear that the old man was not going anywhere until I brought up the question that he knew I wanted to ask.

"Lacey worked pretty good for me today," I mentioned, as I stood back and surveyed my work.

"It looked like she was going pretty well," he added, blowing out a puff of smoke. "How'd she back for you after I left?"

"Well, actually," I started, "I never did get a chance to back her again."

"No?"

"No," I said, with a hint of embarrassment in my voice. "I guess I didn't know what you meant when you said I shouldn't back her with the bit."

I finally looked up at the old man. He was standing with a slight smile on his face. He took a drag from his cigarette, nodded slowly, and motioned for me to follow him into the tack room.

I set my hammer down on the wood pile and followed him through the door, only to find him staring up at a number of bridles hanging on the wall. He reached up and pulled down an old leather headstall with an O-ring snaffle bit. The leather reins were tangled slightly and attached to the bit with Chicago screws. He fumbled with the bit and reins before the tangle was out and then handed me the headstall and bit while he held on to the reins.

"Take the bit in your hand," he said, as the smoke from his cigarette boiled out of his mouth, causing him to squint slightly, "and put the headstall up on your arm."

I lay the leather headstall on my extended right arm with the brow band up over my shoulder and took the bit in my hand, closing my fist around it.

"Okay, now close your eyes and tell me when you first feel me pulling on the bit with the reins."

I closed my eyes and waited. After a few seconds I could feel the bit move, but didn't say anything because I didn't really feel him "pull" on the bit.

"Do you feel anything yet?" he asked.

"Well, no. Yes. Sort of, I guess."

"Which one is it?"

"Um, I guess it's yes. I am feeling something."

"Okay, good." I could feel the bit go back into a relaxed position. "Now this time, as soon as you feel something from the bit I want you to take a step toward the pressure. Understand?"

I nodded and waited for the bit to move again. I felt an ever-so-slight pull on the bit, barely enough to feel, but I was sure it was there. As soon as I felt it (and, of course, wanting to appear the ever-alert student), I took a step forward, toward the pressure.

"Very good," Even with my eyes closed, I could hear the smile in the old man's voice. "Let's try it again."

I relaxed once more and waited for the bit to move. This time it moved even less than it had before, but again, wanting to appear the superior student, I moved toward the pressure as soon as I felt it.

"Good," he said again. "Now tell me something."

I opened my eyes and looked up at him.

"Was I pulling you toward me with the bit?"

"Pulling me?" I was a little bewildered. "No, sir."

"Did you feel like fighting against the pressure?"

"No."

"Was it easy for you to do what I was asking you to do?"

"Yes, sir," I said with a hint of surprise. "It was real easy."

"Well," he said, taking the headstall off my arm and hanging it carefully back on the wall, "it was easy for me, too."

With that, he took the last drag from his cigarette, went to the door, and rolled the end of it between his fingers until the hot cherry had all but disappeared. The remaining tobacco floated to the ground along with the last remnants of the paper that had held it. He stomped the entire thing into the dirt with the toe of his boot and walked out the door.

The very next day I brought Lacey in, brushed and tacked her up, and headed to the round pen for our daily session. We were both in pretty good spirits, as I recall, and it wasn't long before I was mounted up and we were going through our normal routine. Walk forward, turn to the right, turn to the left, stop, sit a few seconds, and then do the whole thing over again. After about five minutes, I decided it was time to try to ask her to back up.

Lacey had stopped very nicely and was standing quietly when I slowly started to take the slack out of the reins. I was trying desperately to be soft and quiet, just as the old man had been when he backed her the day before and when he'd worked with me in the barn.

At first, even though I was using very light pressure, I didn't feel like I was getting any response whatsoever from the mare. In fact, I was just getting ready to start applying more pressure when an idea suddenly popped into my mind. When the old man had me try to feel when he was putting pressure on the bit I was holding, he had me close my eyes. Now granted, I didn't know if that was so I couldn't see when he was applying pressure or if it was so that I could truly feel what he was doing. Either way, I think it was an important piece of the puzzle that I'd missed, and so, as I sat in the saddle and took the slack from Lacey's reins, I simply closed my eyes.

Just like that, I was suddenly feeling things through the reins that I hadn't felt before. There was a little brace here, a little give there, a slight jiggle of the bit, a tipping of her nose, a little bending at the poll—all within a few seconds. I released the pressure briefly, then picked it up once again to feel another wide variety of movements through the reins. Without warning, while I was busy trying to decipher all the movement I detected through the reins, I felt a completely different motion from Lacey. It was a shift of her weight backward! Not much of a shift, mind you. In fact, had I been *looking* for it, I don't think I would have ever felt it. But I think the fact that I had my eyes closed forced me to feel it.

Immediately I released what little pressure I was applying to the reins, opened my eyes, and leaned forward to pet her on her neck. I sat quietly for a few seconds and tried again. I closed my eyes, took a little slack from the reins, and as soon as I felt contact on her mouth, simply waited. I believe less than six seconds passed before I was once again feeling a number of very light responses from her. Less than ten seconds passed before I felt another shift of her weight backwards, and immediately I released the pressure. I did this three more times when, suddenly and with hardly any pressure applied to the bit, she took several steps backward!

Shocked that the mare had moved backward with such light pressure, I just about threw my reins down. I excitedly scanned the area for the old man, hoping that he had seen what we'd just done, but he was nowhere to be seen. I regained my composure and went back to working with Lacey in the same way. In less than five minutes she was backing five, ten, fifteen steps at a time with such light pressure that I could hardly believe it was possible. But sure enough, there it was!

Later that day I excitedly told the old man what Lacey and I had accomplished and, as usual, I didn't get much of a response from him. He sat, patiently listening to what I had to say, nodding quietly from time to time but seemingly unimpressed by what I was saying. I remember that he waited until I was done talking and then lit a cigarette. He blew the first puff of smoke from between his lips, settled back in his chair, and looked out the window toward the pasture.

"Any time you're willing to fight with horses," he said in a low, unwavering tone, "they'll always be willing to fight back. The thing is, though, even during those fights the horse is still trying to figure out what you want. The sad part is, because you're so busy fighting with them, you'll never feel those tries. Sounds to me like you finally quit fighting with her."

At the time, those were just words to me. They didn't seem to have much meaning behind them. Perhaps it was because I was still pretty young or perhaps because I was still caught up in the moment of what had happened between myself and Lacey. Either way, it would be years before I fully understood the importance of what the old man had said to me that day.

I'd been asked to ride the young gelding for a simple reason, to get him to willingly make transitions from one gait to the next. We had been at it for nearly an hour-and-a-half, and oddly enough, we weren't any farther ahead than when we started. All I could think of was that it shouldn't have to be this hard.

Granted, this was a pretty green horse—he'd only been started about forty-five days before—but still, he seemed to be having more trouble than most trying to understand what was being asked of him. Nothing I did seemed to have any impact on him, and in fact, the more pressure I put on him to move forward, the less he actually moved. It had gotten to the point where we were making small circles in the middle of the arena at a very slow walk, if we moved at all.

The owner had been standing near the fence the entire time and was beginning to show her frustration at my lack of ability to get her horse to respond. I couldn't really blame her, because frankly I was getting pretty frustrated myself. I was beginning to feel as though there was nothing that I could do to get the horse to do what I was asking. I had tried everything I knew, including squeezing him with my heels, kicking him, slapping him with the reins, squirming around in the saddle so that it was uncomfortable for him to stand still—everything that I could think of—and nothing had worked. In fact, I could feel that my frustration was beginning to get the better of me. What's worse, I felt my thought process begin to shut down, and in its place was a sort of primeval desire to *make* this horse respond, no matter what the cost. It wasn't a feeling I liked, and it took everything I had to keep from giving in to it.

I decided to take a break. I climbed off the gelding and led him over to his owner.

"Are you quitting?" she asked, the frustration evident in her voice.

"Not yet," I told her. "Just taking a break for a few minutes."

"This is how he's been since I got him back from the trainer," she said in disgust. "He told me he'd get better with these transitions, but he's only gotten worse. Maybe you should put some spurs on. That's what the other trainer did."

"I'd rather not do that if I can help it," I said, as I reached over and petted the gelding on the head.

"I just don't understand why this has to be such a fight," she shook her head. "I'd think it would be easier for him just to do it, but he doesn't even try."

Suddenly it hit me, right between the eyes—the words the old man had spoken to me all those years ago about fighting with horses came back as if he were standing right in front of me. No wonder I couldn't get this little guy to respond to me ... heck, I'd been fighting with him the entire time. Even if he had been trying to do what I was asking of him, there was no way I could tell because I was doing so much *to* him that I wouldn't have been able to feel it. All this time I had been looking for the *big* thing from this horse—the transition itself. By doing so, however, I had missed the one little thing that would ultimately make the transition possible—the try. Before we could get the transition, I first needed to feel him trying to make the transition. In order for me to feel the try, one thing was certain—I needed to back off and lighten up.

I gave myself a few minutes to kind of catch my breath and then took the gelding back out to the middle of the arena and mounted up. This time, I was ready to go at the entire thing with a different attitude. Instead of trying to *make* him respond to my cues, I would let him try to figure out the right answer. More importantly, I was more willing to feel when he was offering to do the right thing. I would take what he could give and simply go from there.

After mounting up, I asked the gelding to move forward by kissing to him and applying just a little leg to his sides. This time I felt something from him that I hadn't felt before. It was sort of a surge forward for a step or two. It wasn't a big surge, mind you. It was more like a wave had picked him up from behind and pushed him forward. After only a step or two, it felt as if the wave receded and the push was gone. I let him take another couple of steps, applied a little leg, and kissed to him again. Again there was a surge forward and again, after only a few steps, the surge receded.

It dawned on me that perhaps these little surges were his tries and I had been looking past them. If these surges were in fact the try I had been hoping for, maybe all I needed to do to build towards a transition was to work with him just as I had with Lacey all those years ago. I needed to acknowledge the try by making sure I released my cue on time and build on the try by reapplying the cue before the forward surge was completely gone.

I asked for a little more forward movement with the squeeze and kiss, and once again I felt the surge. As soon as I felt an increase in his forward movement, I released the cues, but this time I applied another cue before the surge receded. Almost immediately I felt another surge and, just as quickly, I released the cue. He picked up a little faster walk and sustained it for three or four steps before I began to feel a slight loss of momentum. Once again I applied a squeeze and a kiss, he picked up his pace, and I released the cue. This went on for the next few minutes. Each time I applied a cue and released, his steps became quicker and he was able to sustain the livelier movement for longer periods.

Before I knew it, the slow walk that had seemed our only option just a short time before was turning into this very fluid, energy-filled forward movement. The gelding's entire body was moving much freer, and he was much more focused and a whole lot more willing. On top of all that, I wasn't even having to use leg cues anymore. A simple kissing sound when I began to feel a loss of momentum was enough to get him to pick the pace back up.

We continued around the arena at a pretty quick walk for a couple of laps before I decided to ask for a transition to the trot. When I did, I simply used my original cue—a little squeeze with my leg and a kissing sound. I felt a big surge from the gelding without hesitation, and I released the cue. Before he could slow the surge, I quickly reapplied the cue and received another, even bigger surge. Another release and one more soft cue, and the gelding moved from a very quick walk right up into a pretty little trot. He traveled quietly, trotting for thirty or forty feet when I suddenly felt him building momentum again. However, this was a different kind of momentum. Instead of the fluid, focused movement we had in the walk, this was a tight, worried movement.

It was such an uncomfortable departure from what I had been feeling that I decided to get him out of it as quickly as I could. After all, if he was having trouble carrying me in the trot, I certainly didn't want to make things worse by trying to force him to carry me. With that, I relaxed in the saddle, picked up ever so slightly on the reins, and brought him back to a walk. He sighed deeply, dropped his head, and picked up a fast walk.

We traveled in the walk for about half a lap before I asked once again for a trot. This time I kissed to him but tried not to use my legs as an additional cue. He surged forward, but didn't get the trot, so I added the squeeze when I reapplied the cue. That time he picked up the trot without hesitation. After thirty or forty feet, before he became concerned, I asked him to return to the walk, and he went back to being quiet and relaxed.

This went on for about five minutes before he was able to settle into the trot for longer and longer periods of time. Soon I was able to ask for the trot with a very light cue, often just a kissing sound, get the transition within just a few feet, and let him travel in it quietly for as long as he was comfortable. With each transition he seemed to gain more and more confidence in both me and himself, and he was soon trotting entire laps around the arena without becoming concerned in the least.

Even though he was more relaxed in the trot itself, what really amazed me was his responsiveness in the transitions. Once I quit fighting with him and began rewarding his efforts to respond to my cues, he became extremely willing to do what I was asking. The fight and confusion just seemed to melt away, and a whole new horse emerged.

This was truly a learning experience for me, not just because we'd had a breakthrough in accomplishing the task at hand (getting a transition from the walk to the trot), but because of the way we had accomplished it. We had gone from an hour-and-a-half of one frustrating fight after another to making soft, quiet transitions within just a matter of minutes. It was almost too good to be true, but sure enough, there it was. Just like that, this horse had single-handedly changed my perception about how and why horses respond to the cues we give them. What an eye-opening experience it was.

After working with that gelding, I made a much bigger effort to look for and find the tries that my horses offered during training or any other time, for that matter. In doing so, I quickly found just how much I had been missing in the simple communication between my horses and myself.

For instance, I noticed that my horses often tried to respond to my cues much sooner than I'd ever imagined. Often times they would respond even before I had actually applied the cue, a pretty scary thought in and of itself.

The other thing I noticed was that very often the try was so subtle that, had I not been paying attention, I would have missed it altogether. As a result, I was forced to become much more aware of what my horses were doing at all times, not just when I was asking something from them.

People often ask me what, in my opinion, constitutes a try from the horse when a cue is given. Well, that's a tough one. It's been my experience that a try can be anything from a flying lead change to the flick of an ear, depending on the circumstance and the horse.

Once I had a horse that was having trouble stopping when pressure was applied to the bit. Each time you picked up on the reins, the horse's first response was to jut his nose forward and brace against the pressure. After traveling twenty feet or so, he would finally plow to a stop. There was never any softness, though.

When I first started working with him, we would be walking along and I would ask him to stop, first by shifting my weight back in the saddle a little, then by lightly picking up on the reins. At first all I could feel from him was more forward movement instead of less. But as time went on, I started to feel him trying to figure out what I was asking of him. I felt a slight loss of momentum just after

I shifted my weight in the saddle and touched the reins. If this loss of momentum was, in fact, his try, then I needed to make sure that I rewarded him for that try.

The next time I asked for a stop and felt the small loss of momentum, I immediately rewarded him with a slight release of the pressure from the reins. He still didn't stop, though, so I reapplied the pressure and again felt another loss of momentum. I released and again the stop didn't come. However, on the next try, the stop did come and the brace was much less noticeable. After we stopped, I released the pressure, let him think about it for a second or two, then picked up the reins and asked him to back.

I took up just enough slack so that I could feel contact with his mouth and waited. In a few seconds, I could feel him trying to figure out a way to rid himself of the pressure, even though the pressure was very light. He jutted his nose forward. No release. He tossed his head up. No release. He braced against the bit and dropped his head. No release. He turned his head from one side to the other. No release. Finally he stood with his head forward, flexed slightly at the poll, and began sort of rolling the bit quietly in his mouth. Ah. That was it, a try.

Even though he didn't actually attempt to move backward, there was a softening that wasn't there before. He needed to soften before we could back, and that was what he'd given me. I immediately released the pressure as a reward. He softened even more. I picked up the reins and reapplied the same light pressure. Once again he went through a number of things to rid himself of the pressure but found the one thing that helped was softening through the poll and holding the bit quietly in his mouth.

After that, each time I picked up the pressure he got softer and softer until finally, after about five minutes, I felt him actually think about moving backward. When I say he was thinking about backing, that's just what I mean. There was a little movement, but it was just a twitch of a muscle—a sort of question from him, as if he were asking, *Is this what you're looking for?*

On the next attempt, the "thought" was even bigger. Instead of just a twitch, there was more of a shift. It still wasn't the whole horse, mind you, but the try was definitely getting bigger. The next time, the shift became a drift, and on the next attempt, the drift became a step. One step quickly became two, two became four, and four became eight, all on a very light rein with no bracing from him whatsoever.

We continued to work on stopping and backing for the next thirty minutes or so, and with each stop and back, he became lighter and lighter. By the time we quit for the day, he was no longer bracing against the bit during his stops, and his backing had become light as a feather. All, I believe, because *his* idea of what a try was had been noticed and then rewarded.

One of the biggest problems I see when working with folks and their horses is that the vast majority of people have been trained to always look for the bad things their horses do. Because they're always looking for the bad, they easily overlook the little tries and sometimes have trouble seeing the good in their horse, even when the good jumps up and bites them in the butt.

A few years back I was asked to help a fellow get his Arab gelding to do flying lead changes. Now, this particular gelding was an ex-show horse and had performed trouble-free flying lead changes for over five years. The man had bought the horse a year or so before and hadn't gotten a flying lead change out of him since.

When the pair came into the arena, it was clear, at least to me, that the fellow had somewhat of a chip on his shoulder. He wasn't happy with the horse at all and had a pretty sour attitude toward the gelding.

"I think I was sold a bill of goods," the man told me. "I've been trying to get these lead changes from him since I bought him, but he just refuses to do 'em. He's pretty pig-headed."

"Well, lets have a look," I shrugged. "Maybe he's just having trouble understanding what you want."

"Oh, he knows what I want, all right," the man grunted. "He just doesn't want to do it."

"Well," I said, "how about if we just start at the beginning and see what we come up with?" The man mounted up and immediately began trotting and then loping around the arena. At first I thought he was just warming up. I saw that wasn't the case, as he loped the horse across the middle of the arena on the left lead, then suddenly threw his weight to the right and jerked the reins in the same direction in an attempt to get a flying lead change. Taken by surprise and thrown completely off balance, the horse's head popped up, and he immediately dropped from the lope to a trot. That infuriated the man, who kicked the gelding hard in the ribs. The gelding responded by wringing his tail, throwing a halfhearted crow hop, and finally picking up his right lead.

"See what I mean!" the man yelled across the arena. "He just doesn't want to do it."

Well, I guess that was one way to look at it. The other way to look at it was that there was no way the horse could change leads when he was thrown that far out of balance. One thing was certain just from the little bit I had seen—the horse was not only well trained, he also seemed pretty willing to do what was asked of him.

That was evident in his willingness to make transitions, which he did flawlessly, as well as in his attempt to take the right lead, even after he had been so unceremoniously knocked nearly off his feet by his rider.

I asked the man to come back around so that we could start over, taking things just a little slower. He brought the gelding over and I explained that I thought his horse would probably do the lead changes for him, providing we could set him up properly and then get out of his way so that he could do them. It was evident by the look on his face that the man was having trouble understanding what I meant. I went on to explain that we were going to slow down and let both of them warm up to the idea of switching leads, instead of just jumping in the middle and hoping for the best. Surprisingly enough, the man agreed with the idea and soon he was back out in the arena.

The first thing we needed to do was get the two of them on the same page, so to speak. I asked that they start in a trot and move in large circles in the middle of the arena, first in one direction, then cutting across the middle of the arena and reversing direction, effectively making a large figure eight as they traveled. Each time they crossed the center and reversed direction, I asked the man to cue his horse as softly as he could, as if he was asking for a lead change, even though they were still only at the trot. At first, the man's cues were big and obtrusive. He was applying a heavy outside leg accompanied by jerking on the reins. However, the more he worked, the lighter his cues got. Before long he was no longer jerking on the reins, and his heavy leg cue had turned into nothing more than a quiet shift of his weight.

When it was clear that he was ready to move up into the lope, I asked him to make his transition, but go only clockwise. He kindly asked the horse for the transition, and the horse responded flaw-lessly by picking up its right lead and traveling quietly in a circle. They made about four laps before I asked the man to slow the horse to a trot, give the soft cue for a lead change, and reverse directions the next time they came across the center. Once they were traveling in a counterclockwise circle, I asked that the pair pick up the lope, which they did effortlessly. I had them reverse directions a couple more times, each time slowing to a trot as they came across the center, cuing for the lead change, and picking up the correct lead.

After fifteen minutes of this, something very interesting began to happen. As the pair were loping in a clockwise circle and coming across the middle, the gelding began to drift toward the counter-clockwise circle. The man straightened the gelding out and contin-ued through the clockwise circle. However, the next time he came across the middle the gelding once again began to lean toward the counterclockwise circle. This time the man pulled the gelding to a stop.

"Dang it," the man yelled. "See how he's dumping his shoul-der? He's pulling me out of the circle."

"Is he pulling you out of the circle," I asked, "or is he doing something else?"

"What do you mean?"

"Well," I suggested, "we've been getting him ready to do a fly-ing lead change right along. Maybe he's trying to tell us he's ready."

"So you're telling me that him dumping his shoulder is his way of telling me he can do a flying lead change?"

"I don't know," I told him. "But maybe if we let him try, we'll find out."

It was clear that the man wasn't convinced. To be hon-est, neither was I. But it seemed pretty funny to me that a horse comfortably traveling in one direction in the lope would suddenly *want* to pull off in the other direction for no apparent reason. That didn't make sense either.

So, with that, the man went back out and started the entire exercise over again. Within a few minutes he had worked up to the lope and was traveling in a clockwise circle. After about three laps, the gelding began to pull toward the counterclockwise circle as they came across the middle. At that point, the man quietly turned the gelding toward the left, and just like that, the gelding breezed into his left lead without missing a step. The pair came back around, and as they crossed the center, the man leaned slightly to the right and his horse breezed into his right lead.

The interesting thing about this situation was that the horse had not only tried to do what was being asked of him, he also tried to tell us that he knew what we wanted. On top of that, he even tried to tell us when he was ready to do it! Had we looked at his pulling into the turn as simply "dumping his shoulder," we would have missed his entire effort to communicate all of this to us.

As I said, many folks have been trained to look for just the bad things that horses do and therefore sometimes have a very hard time finding the good. The problem with looking at horses in such a way is that even when our horse is trying his best to be good and making an effort to do the right thing, we might never see it. Because we are constantly looking for the big thing (the flawless lead change, the effortless transition, the sliding stop), we often look right past the most important part—the try that tells us our horse is understanding our request. Horses are such subtle animals that even the flick of an ear, the softening of the jaw, or the twitch of a muscle all mean something to them. Very often it is those simple little things that are at the very heart of the big things that we look to get from them, but because we look right past them, we never even know they're there. As a result, our horses often become frustrated with us, we become frustrated with them, and the trust between us becomes damaged.

It seems to me that by searching for, finding, and then acknowledging those little tries, we are opening a whole new door to communication that will ultimately help our horses look to us as responsible, fair, and dependable leaders for them.

In the end, I expect that is all they would ask from us anyway, if they could.

NOTES FOR FINDING THE TRY

All three of my kids are out of high school now and on to other things in their lives. An interesting note is that just before they all graduated, a big manila envelope arrived in the mail for each one. In the envelope, among other things, was a letter that each one wrote to themselves back when they were in seventh grade. They all had the same seventh grade teacher, and as a project at the end of their seventh grade year, this teacher had them write a letter to their future self that would be given to them when they graduated. In the letters, they talked about all the things that were important to them in seventh grade, who their friends were, what their interests were, what they wanted to do in the future, etc., and then they asked what they were doing now that they were graduating seniors. It was an interesting concept . . . to have your own voice talking to you from the past.

That's how I have begun to look at the books I have written. Each one is a snapshot of where I once was, and in re-reading what I wrote years ago, it gives me a glimpse back in time to what I was doing and thinking and working on at the time—and where I wanted to go in the future. In reading this chapter on Finding the Try, I can clearly see the path I was going down then, and continue to go down to this day.

I remember when originally writing this chapter that I was trying to make the point that a horse's "try" to do what we are asking is often much smaller than we might think, and is almost always smaller than what we are looking for. In the years since writing this book, and in particular this chapter, I have come to understand that a horse's "try" is very often even smaller than what I understood it to be back then!

Horses have the innate ability to communicate on a level I'm not sure we humans completely understand and that we may never be able to achieve. However, one thing I know for sure is that if we don't try to get to their level, we absolutely will never get there. My goal when writing this chapter originally was to get folks thinking about searching for responses from their horses on a slightly more subtle level than perhaps what they may have been looking for at the time. As I re-read this chapter now, it is a great reminder from my former self to my present self to also continue along that same path of trying to find the ultimate in subtle communication.

Half a Chance

Trust is a funny thing. We all want to be trusted and, in fact, often feel offended at the mere hint that someone else doesn't trust us . . . even if that person is someone we just met. Yet we find it perfectly acceptable to balk at putting our trust in others. Yes, before we can trust someone else, that person must first prove that they *can* be trusted. There'll be no willy-nilly giving away of our trust, that's for sure.

It all has to do with our suspicious nature. Most folks are kind of funny that way. Not that that's a bad thing, mind you. I expect that's what has kept our species alive and kicking for so long. Still, it's an interesting dilemma . . . wanting to be trusted but not necessarily wanting to trust.

Now, let's throw a horse into the equation. Most of us are constantly searching for a relationship with our horse that is based on trust. In theory, we want to trust our horse and we want our horse to trust us. In reality, however, what we usually have is a sort of one-way trust. In other words, we trust that our horse trusts us, but we don't really trust our horse.

Even with my horse Buck—a horse that I *thought* I trusted with my life—I found that when push came to shove and he needed me to trust his judgment, I turned on him and relied more on my own judgment than his.

It happened a few years back. A young horse arrived for training and had been unloaded into one of the corrals down near the driveway. He was a nice-looking bay gelding but came with a little baggage. Specifically, he had been abused and was pretty doggone leery of people. He was difficult to catch and wasn't real sociable with the other horses. The corral had a gate that opened into the driveway, near the old blue trailer that we used to cart away manure.

Once he was unloaded, we decided to give the gelding a few days to settle in before we asked anything of him. We usually did that as a matter of course anyway, but it seemed particularly important for this little guy due to his fragile state of mind. After getting him settled in the pen and making sure he had enough feed and water, I decided the day was still pretty young, so I saddled up old Buck and he and I went for a ride.

Not long after we started out, the weather turned threatening, like it wanted to rain, so after being out for about an hour, we turned around and headed back to the home place. As we came up the driveway, way, I noticed that the pen where the new gelding had been seemed to be awfully empty. Not only that, but the gate to the pen was standing half open. That struck me as odd because I could distinctly remember closing the gate and latching it myself after feeding the gelding. I also remembered looking at the gate when Buck and I went past as we headed out for our ride, and I knew for certain that gate had been closed and latched.

As we got closer, I noticed my young son, Tyler, who was four years old at the time, in the corral with a scoop shovel. Now Tyler was a pretty conscientious little boy, even at that early age, and helped out around the place whenever he thought he could. One of his favorite things to do in the world was clean the horse pens, which he did with me every morning. However, on that particular morning, Tyler had slept in. I'd gone out before he'd awakened and cleaned the pens by myself. Needless to say, he wasn't very happy with me for leaving him out of the daily ritual.

After I left on my ride, Tyler noticed that the new horse's pen had a little manure in it. So, seeing as how he'd missed out on the morning cleaning, he decided to go in and scoop the pen so it would be nice and clean when I got back. Unfortunately, in his enthusiasm to get the pen cleaned, he accidentally left the gate ajar, and the new gelding promptly made his getaway.

By the time Buck and I returned, the gelding was long gone. After thanking Tyler for cleaning the pen and mentioning to him that perhaps next time he might want to close the gate, I grabbed a halter, lead rope, and lariat, climbed back on Buck, and headed out to see if we could track the gelding down.

We quickly picked up the gelding's tracks near the side of the road and followed them to a large field about a mile down the road. At one time it was just a big open space at the foot of the mountain, but in recent years it had begun to fill up with houses. Buck was the first to see the gelding. Riding into the grass, he suddenly snapped to attention and looked toward a bunch of trees near the other end of the field. Off in the distance was a small brown clump that looked like a dirt pile to me, but Buck knew different.

We began riding toward the clump; it wasn't long before the outline of a horse began to take shape, and I knew right away that Buck had been correct. We were within about a hundred yards of the gelding when he noticed us. His head popped out of the grass and he trotted up to us to investigate. He and Buck sniffed noses for a short time; then the gelding turned, trotted off a short distance, and stopped, almost as if to say, *All right, come on and catch me so we can go back home.*

The gelding was a little nervous but seemed unwilling to get too far away from Buck. Seeing that, I climbed down and started toward him, leading Buck as I went. As soon as I hit the ground, however, the gelding became more nervous and suddenly trotted off. I remounted and trailed him, making sure not to appear as if we were chasing him. We just sort of headed in the same direction he was moving. We stopped when he stopped and moved when he moved but, other than that, we tried to be in no real hurry to approach him. After about half an hour, by working slowly, we had worked up to within a few feet of him. That time I stayed mounted and asked Buck to slowly side pass up alongside the gelding. We side passed because I figured we would appear less threatening to him than if we had approached headlong toward him. This seemed to work for him, because as we made our way over, one or two steps at a time, he never offered to run off.

A few minutes passed before we were able to get right alongside the gelding, and I took a great deal of time slowly reaching down and petting him to let him know I wanted him to stay. He was pretty relaxed before long, and I figured it was as good a time as any to halter him up. I carefully took the halter I had draped over the saddle horn and rubbed him quietly on the neck with it. He seemed unconcerned, so I decided to reach over and slip the halter on him. I had leaned down from the saddle and opened the nose band of the halter so that I could slide it on him, when the back door of a nearby house swung open and a lady with two kids came trotting out.

"Hi, there!" she yelled, in a big, friendly voice. "Can we pet your horses?"

Well, this sudden flurry of activity was a little more than the gelding could stand, and the woman hadn't even finished her sentence before he bolted forward and literally headed for the hills at top speed. Just about then—as we watched the southbound end of that northbound horse disappear up the long trail that headed toward the top of the nearby mountain—I figured we might be in for a pretty long afternoon.

The only thing I could think, as I forced the thin mountain air in and out of my lungs, was that this hill was sure a whole lot steeper than it looked. The trail was very rocky and pretty washed out and ran nearly straight up and down just to one side of a power line, which was more than likely the only reason anyone would have put a trail here to begin with. I had stayed on Buck as long as I thought was prudent but chose to get off about halfway up. It was just too dang steep to ask him to carry me all the way.

We were still a ways from the top, and the gelding was grazing in the tall grass just to the right of the trail. We had gotten pretty close to him a time or two, but each time he bolted and ran farther up the hill. As we neared him this time, he turned and trotted off once again, disappearing up and over the top of the hill.

Buck and I finally reached the crest, and after taking a minute or two to catch my breath, I mounted up and we started down the trail on the other side of the mountain. Luckily for us, the trail didn't go straight down the mountain but meandered its way down a gentle slope through the trees and rocks. This trail was actually part of a system of trails used by a local livery stable located near the bottom of the mountain. I took this as especially good luck for Buck and me, because I knew that the trail would end up right at the livery's barn, where there would more than likely be wranglers around just finishing up their day. Surely they would catch my loose horse and wait for someone to come around and pick him up. At that point I was thinking that Buck and I had it made and that we'd be back home before supper.

About fifteen minutes into our downward trek, we ran into something that I hadn't expected. Just in front of us the trail branched off in two directions. One branch led back up the side of the mountain to the right, the other headed down and to the left. At first, I was concerned about which way we should go, but my concern quickly faded, because it was pretty clear which branch of the trail our little horse would have chosen.

The trail to the right was undeveloped and got steep right off the bat. I didn't see any sign that our horse had passed that way . . . no tracks, manure, or the like. The trail to the left was well worn and continued the gentle downward slope we'd been traveling. There were also tracks and fresh manure scattered down the middle of the trail that looked as if it may have been left there within the last few minutes. As far as I was concerned, this was a no-brainer—we needed to go left.

Buck, on the other hand, had a different idea. We had no sooner reached the split in the trail than he turned and headed straight up the hill to the right. Surprised, I asked him to stop and, because there wasn't enough room to turn around, asked him to back down the way we'd just come. Oddly enough, he refused. It was not like Buck to refuse a request, and I guess I should have known right then and there that something was up, but I let it pass and continued to ask him to back. He refused, standing planted in one spot, leaning on the bit. I tipped his nose slightly and asked again for him to back. He refused.

"Come on, Buck," I heard myself say. "We're wasting time here."

Buck blew hard through his nose and shook his head, as if he was getting pretty aggravated with me. I dismissed it as him being a little tired from the two-and-a-half hours we'd already spent chasing the gelding and asked again for him to back. He snorted even harder, shook his head defiantly one last time, and backed grudgingly down to the trail junction.

I turned him down the trail to the left and urged him forward. He balked, focusing all his attention to the right and letting out a long whinny back up the mountain.

"I'm telling you, Buck," I reassured him, "there's no way he went up there."

Buck pawed the dirt hard three or four times, snorted, and shook his head. I let him have his little temper tantrum and urged him downward. He gave in, but not before sending me a heartfelt snort and one last head shake. He carried me down the hill, but it was clear from the first step that he wasn't happy doing it. He put his feet down as though he was mad at the ground the entire way down, and his periodic snorts and head shakes were a good indicator that he wasn't pleased with my decision.

It didn't really matter, though, because I was as sure as I could be that when we got to the livery stable at the bottom of the mountain, the gelding would be there, all caught up and waiting for us to take him home. You can imagine my surprise when, about forty-five minutes later, we rode into the livery parking lot and found the gelding was nowhere in sight.

I gave Buck a drink at the water trough, tied him off at a hitch rail, and went into the office, where I inquired about the gelding. No one had seen him. In fact, the last trail ride of the day had just returned to the barn, having been on the same trail I'd ridden in on, and they hadn't seen any sign of the horse.

I was in a dilemma. The sun would soon be down, which would make searching for the horse in the mountains next to impossible, and Buck was nearly played out. Heading back up the trail to the fork where Buck had wanted to turn off was out of the question. He was too tired, and if I led him up the trail, it would take nearly an hour-and-a-half just to get to the turnoff. I asked to borrow one of the livery horses to continue my search, but it was the busy season for them and all their horses were tired from packing dudes all day. I was fairly despondent over the entire situation, but I left my name with the livery manager, who promised that her staff would keep a watch out for the gelding throughout the night. After all, if he were still on the mountain, he was likely to find a trail and follow it down to the livery anyway.

Feeling that I'd done all I could do, I mounted, and Buck and I dejectedly walked out to the road, where we headed for home. The road looped its way around for a couple miles and met up with another road that would put us right back in front of the house.

We were only about a quarter-mile from home, with the sun beginning to set and the cool of the early evening settling in, when Buck snapped to attention and stared off to the right toward the mountain we had just spent the last four-and-a-half hours on. We had begun at the eastern foot of the mountain, climbed up through a saddle bridging the eastern and western slopes, traversed down the western side of the mountain and around to the north, to the livery. Finally, we circled back around to the northeast, where we were standing.

I looked out into the dusk across a pasture fenced on three sides and, to my surprise, standing right there at what appeared to be an old forgotten trailhead covered with downed timber and brush, was the gelding. He was certainly no worse for the wear and was grazing quietly, as if he owned the place.

Buck called loudly to him and snorted, shaking his head with a vigor I hadn't seen since we'd had our discussion about which trail to take. The gelding heard him and called back. He came toward us starting at a walk, moving into a trot, and finally working up to an all-out lope. He rapidly covered the ground between us and pulled up right next to Buck, as if to say, *Hey, where you been?*

Just as I had done hours before, I asked Buck to side pass up to the gelding while I pulled the halter from the saddle horn. We were able to get right up to him, and this time, as if it were what he'd been waiting for the entire time, he let me slip the halter over his nose and buckle it in place. I guess the gelding had had enough excitement for one day, too. Just like that, our ordeal was over, and the three of us were soon making our way back home as darkness began to hide the mountain.

The next day I saddled Buck and we went over to the place he'd spotted the gelding the night before, near the old hidden trailhead. The trailhead was on private property, which was one of the reasons I'd never been on it before. After getting permission, we rode through. It took a little doing, but we were able to get up on the trail and follow it back around the side of the mountain. The trail went up a gradual slope for about half a mile,

through an open meadow, circled back through the woods to the northwest, and finally met up with the trail we'd been on the day before at the junction where Buck and I had had our discussion. It was less than a mile from where we caught the gelding the night before. It took just under thirty minutes to get from the old trailhead to the junction—but it will take a lifetime for me to live it down.

All I could do was shake my head and stroke Buck on the neck in a feeble attempt at an apology for not listening to him when we both knew I should have. Because I wasn't willing to put my trust in Buck when it counted, I ended up putting both of us through more grief than was necessary, not to mention wasting nearly two hours worth of daylight and putting the gelding in undue danger because we weren't able to get to him sooner. Had I just trusted that Buck knew what he was doing when he tried to take me up that trail, we could have avoided all that.

Unfortunately, we humans are simply not programmed to think that way. We're programmed to think that we're smarter than our horses and that our decisions are *always* the right ones . . . for both of us. Over the past several years, it has come to me that, perhaps, in order for our horses to truly look to us as a leader, there needs to be some give and take in the relationship we have with them. In other words, perhaps we need to give them half a chance from time to time, so we can show them that their judgment in certain situations can, in fact, be trusted. At the very least, we can communicate to them that we are willing to meet them halfway—even in situations where their judgment may leave a little to be desired.

It had been going on now for quite some time, and it was beginning to be a little aggravating for me. I had been working with the mare for about three weeks and, overall, things were going pretty well. However, she had one little quirk that didn't seem to improve no matter how much I worked with her—anytime we were riding in the arena, traveling along the rail, she would abruptly, for no apparent reason, start pulling off the rail toward the center of the arena.

It wasn't a big pull; it wasn't a big fight. It was more like a request. We'd be going along just as nice as could be, and suddenly she would start leaning toward the inside, first with her inside shoulder, and finally with a slight turn in her neck, Each time I nicely tipped her nose toward the rail, but that didn't seem to help. After a while I began to add a little inside leg to urge her back, and eventually she'd wander her way to the rail. But she would never stay there. Usually less than half a lap later she would be pulling me to the inside again, and we would start the whole process over.

After about three weeks of this, she still wasn't any better at staying on the rail than when we had first started. I had her checked for physical ailments, teeth problems, ill-fitting tack, and foot problems—and everything checked out just fine. I worked hard to ride her in a very conscientious manner to make sure that I wasn't inadvertently causing her to come off the rail because of the way I was sitting in the saddle. That didn't seem to be it, either. After a couple weeks of close examination, I finally came to the conclusion that the reason she was pulling away from the rail was because she was expressing an opinion. She didn't want to be on the rail.

We were approaching an impasse. I needed her on the rail in order to get some of our work accomplished, and she didn't want to be there. What could I do about it? I could force her to stay on

146

the rail with little trouble, but if I did that, where would the trust be? I wanted her to stay on the rail because it was her decision to do so, not because I wasn't giving her any other choice, yet I still wanted to get the task accomplished with the least amount of stress on both of us and without making her feel forced into the decision.

I gave the matter a great deal of thought, trying to come up with an idea that would be easy to perform and yet be meaningful enough to the mare that she would *want* to stay on the rail for me. In the end, the idea I came up with had very little to do with a specific training technique and everything to do with giving the mare the benefit of the doubt and actually using her desire to come off the rail to my benefit.

I tried it about fifteen minutes into one of our rides. We had walked, trotted, and loped a few laps around the arena when the mare began to turn off the rail. As was my custom, I gently asked her back to the rail by tipping her nose to the outside. She leaned on the bit and pulled harder to the inside. Usually I would apply a little inside leg in order to get her to drift back to the rail, but that time I didn't.

Instead, I allowed her to do what she had wanted to do. I softened my outside rein, and she turned her head to the inside, bringing her entire body off the rail. As soon as her head began to turn, however, I started taking the slack out of the inside rein. I tipped her nose to the inside and asked her to move from the walk to a trot, causing her to make a big sweeping circle just off the rail. We trotted around the circle until we found ourselves right back on the rail in almost the same spot we'd started from. I straightened her head, brought her back to the walk, and asked her to travel down the rail once again.

At first I think we were both a little surprised. It took less than a couple of seconds, but in that short period of time, we had both done exactly what we wanted to do. She got to go to the inside, and I got to go back to the rail.

We traveled nearly the entire length of the arena before she asked again to leave the rail. I asked her to stay by tipping her nose to the outside, and she leaned on me to go to the inside. So, we did the whole thing over again. I released the outside rein, she turned to the inside; I tipped her nose to the inside and asked her to trot. We circled around and were back on the rail in about four seconds. I asked her to walk, straightened her nose, and headed down the rail.

Again, I think we were both surprised at just how easy the whole thing had been. No muss, no fuss, and most importantly, no fight. We continued along the rail, this time for an entire lap, before she asked if she could go to the inside. I tipped her nose to the outside, she pulled, and we went through the process again and ended up back on the rail without any fight. We made about a lap-and-a-half before she asked if she could go to the inside again, but this time all it took was me tipping her nose to the outside to convince her to quietly stay. It was the last time that day that she asked to move away from the rail.

Working in the arena over the next two or three days, there were times when she would ask to go to the inside. Each time I would ask her to stay on the rail by tipping her nose to the outside, and almost every time she complied with my request. The couple of times when she was more adamant about taking me to the inside I would let her, but—you guessed it—it wasn't long before we were right back on the rail again.

What I find most interesting about this situation is that throughout the time we were working on this, she never once fought with me and never became belligerent or mean. Instead, she remained calm and willing. Even when I asked her to trot through the circle to return to the rail, she usually did so without hesitation. I'm not entirely sure what to attribute her passiveness to, but I have a couple of ideas.

Throughout my career working with horses, one thing the old man taught me has remained a constant—if I was willing to fight with a horse, the horse was almost always willing to fight back. The thing was, there were always a couple of problems in fighting with horses. The first was that any time I fought with a horse, it usually ended up being meaningless to the horse in the end. The second was that anytime I argued with a horse, I always seemed to breach whatever trust that horse had in me. It usually took quite a while for me to prove myself trustworthy to the horse afterwards.

With this mare, I simply let her have her say. She wanted to come off the rail. But then I also had my say, which was that I needed her back on the rail as quickly as possible. I truly believe that, because she had initially "gotten her way" (for lack of a better phrase), even though it may have only been for a few seconds, she had no reason to argue with me and, therefore, no reason to fight. Basically, when she asked to come off the rail, I told her, *Sure, let's go.* That defused the situation right from the start. Because I was willing to meet her halfway, I believe it was easier for her in the long run to comply with what was being asked. It took less than an hour-and-a-half over a three-day period to get her to stop asking to come off the rail altogether.

What I tried to do was show the mare that I wasn't interested in demanding that she see me as the dominant member of our partnership, but that I was willing to listen to what she had to say. By the same token, I was telling her that, *Yes*, we could do what she was asking, *but look how much work it creates for the both of us.* Each time she pulled us off the rail, we had to take all those extra steps and ultimately ended up back on the rail anyway. By working in such a way, I let her know that if she would leave the decision up to me, I'd keep us on the rail so we could avoid the extra work. And she ultimately replied, *Maybe that'd be best.*

When I talk about this idea of letting the horse have a little say during training, I generally get the same kind of response from people. It starts with a sort of glazing over of the eyes, then a collective gasp, which culminates in a loud chorus of, "You can't do that!"

These folks are concerned about the old idea that if you give your horse an inch, the horse will take a mile. They'll say that letting a horse have its way is the quickest way for it to become spoiled and disrespectful, and once that happens, you'll have a whole new set of problems on your hands.

We need to slow down and back up just a little, because I am certainly not advocating that we let our horses have the run of the place. Not at all. All I'm saying is that there are times when it's to our advantage (and our horse's advantage) to let him have his say, if for no other reason than to let him get it out of his system.

You see, sometimes we get so hung up on trying to accomplish a certain task with our horse that the horse himself gets lost in the shuffle. Because the horse has a little trouble understanding what is happening or what is being asked of him, he becomes frustrated. Once frustrated, the horse may become fearful or defensive, which we may misunderstand as a lack of try. That may cause a number of reactions on our part. The most common is a sort of no-nonsense, "I say, you do . . . and I mean NOW" mentality that sometimes escalates into a situation that no one really cares to be in. Because this type of confrontation often causes the rider to get physical with the horse in one way or another, the horse's trust in the rider's judgment takes a turn downward, and their relationship often becomes damaged.

I'm not saying that we shouldn't be focused on the task at hand, nor am I saying that we shouldn't have goals with our horses. On the contrary. I believe those things are very important in developing a good, sound relationship between horse and rider. However, I don't think that we should let the task or goal become the end-all to a training session, either. If things aren't going well, maybe it's time to listen to what our horse is trying to tell us. It could very well be that he has the answer to why things aren't going well, and if we give him half a chance, perhaps he'll tell us what that is.

I have seen so many horses almost completely give up on people, simply because the people around them haven't tried to listen when the horses needed them to the most.

It was a few years back, and I had just been hired on to manage and oversee the horse program at a local guest ranch. The program had had its problems in the past, but the staff and I had worked pretty hard during the off-season to bring the place up to snuff and felt that we had a pretty good thing going by the time we opened in the spring of the year.

There were a couple of horses, however, that had trouble fitting into the program. They were extremely fearful of everything and everybody and didn't seem to improve as time passed. One was a gelding named Bud, the other a mare named Missy. Both were extremely kind horses, and we felt it was certainly worthwhile to spend some time working with them. They had both been handled pretty roughly by the previous management and neither had much trust in people nor were they too keen on the idea of being worked with.

It was difficult to get the entire story out of anyone about what had happened to these horses and why they didn't trust people very much, but as the months went on, the pieces of the puzzle finally came together. Bud had been started by the previous manager as a two-year-old, and he was used as a guide horse for the next three years. Because he was very fast, and therefore fun to ride, he had been used almost exclusively for "advanced" rides, which meant that from the time someone climbed on his back until the time they climbed off, Bud was supposed to be running. As a result, he had no idea how to walk when someone was in the saddle. When a person got on him, he immediately began to jig, and when he was asked to move forward, he would do so at a lope.

During the season before I came on board, the manager had decided that Bud needed to learn how to walk, and so a number of things had been done to him to get him to slow down. First, he was put in a tie-down. Then he was put in an eight-inch-shank, high-port curb bit with a chain curb strap. From what I could gather, that hardware did slow him down some, but not in the way that was hoped for. He would still lope everywhere he went, but he only moved forward at the speed of another horse's walk. His head would be tucked to his chest, his neck was lathered within five minutes, and he sounded like a freight train as air was forced in and out of his lungs with every step he took. Everybody who rode him put a death grip on the reins, and he never felt any relief from the pressure being applied to the bit. He never really slowed down, either.

It didn't take long to see that trying to teach Bud to give to the pressure of the bit wasn't likely to work very well. We needed to find another way to get through to him other than continually hauling up on his mouth. With that, we took him into the arena, stripped him of his tie-down and long-shanked curb bit, and put him in a simple, full-cheek snaffle bit.

He was a perfect gentleman as I led him into the arena. In fact, he was flawless in his ground work and showed no sign of the trouble he had when someone was on his back. His calm disappeared as soon as I tightened the cinch and slid my foot into the stirrup. His energy level immediately increased, he began breathing hard, and he flexed at the poll until his head was almost to his chest. I tried to quiet him by stroking him gently on the neck, but he was having none of it. Feeling that the only way to help him, if I could at all, was to get in the saddle and get started, I slowly stepped up and slid into the saddle.

I felt as if I was sitting on the nose cone of a booster rocket, getting ready for blastoff. The amount of energy he put out just standing there was unbelievable, and as I asked him forward, it all went right through the roof. He took off at a dead run and we covered the length of the arena in no time flat. Knowing that pulling back on the reins wasn't going to be much help, I quickly went to plan B—a one-rein stop. I took the slack from my inside rein and asked him to tip his nose, which he did very nicely. There was only one problem—no one told me that he could turn very tight circles at a dead run and never miss a beat. We circled perhaps seventy or eighty times, covering nearly 220 feet, traveling from the southeast corner of the arena to the northwest corner within seconds. He hadn't slowed a step.

Okay. Time for plan C . . . if only I had one. There was no question that we needed to slow this train down, but how were we going to do it? What would be the one thing I could do to let him know that I didn't need him to be moving out as fast as he was? I decided it would be best to let him tell me what was going to work for him. Perhaps the best way to get him to slow down would be to let him do it on his own. After all, it was obvious that nothing I was going to do in the saddle would matter all that much to him. So, I figured that I needed to let him express his opinion, get everything off his chest. After he had gotten himself into a frame of mind where he could pay attention to what I asked, only then would I ask it.

So I let him run. He made lap after lap, running just as fast as his feet would take him. When I felt he was slowing enough to make a turn safely, I reversed him, and we'd be off again. I made absolutely sure that my legs weren't touching him, so he didn't mistake it as a cue from me to go even faster.

After twenty fast-and-furious minutes, he finally began to run out of steam, and I very quietly asked him to slow down by applying light pressure to the bit. It was as though he never felt it. I asked him three or four times to give to the pressure of the bit, but he never responded. So I began asking a little bit more from him. As we traveled along the rail, I asked him to do a few figure eights and serpentines. He didn't slow much at first, but he did them with as much responsiveness as he could muster. After ten minutes of alternating between the two patterns, his energy level had dropped dramatically, and once again I asked him to drop out of the canter by softening my seat and touching him with the reins. This time, much to my surprise, he slowed from the lope to a trot. I touched him again and he went from the trot to a walk. And finally he stopped.

He was breathing hard and sweating badly, but at least he was stopped. Not wanting him to mistake any movement from me as a cue that I wanted him to move again, I sat as still as I possibly could for the next four or five minutes. Finally, I reached down and petted him on the neck. For the first time, he lowered his head and began licking his lips.

Over the next several weeks, I worked with Bud in pretty much the same way . . . by letting him work through the things he needed to before asking anything of him. Once he did, he could pay attention to and actually perform the tasks I asked of him.

I would love to sit here and tell you that he was 100 percent back to being a good, usable horse after just a few weeks, but unfortunately, that wasn't the case. The truth of the matter is, it took nearly two months before he learned that it was okay for him to walk when someone was on his back. It took another couple of weeks to teach him how to stop with a light cue and still another two months to teach him how to trot and lope without blowing sky high. But the fact remains that once it was all said and done, he became extremely quiet and willing to do whatever was asked of him. Two summers after we first began working with Bud, he was not only safely guiding rides again, but we actually put him back out in the arena, teaching people how to ride. He was one of our top lesson horses.

Missy had a different story. She was an older mare and estimates put her anywhere between twenty-four and fifty-five years old. A nicer mare I don't think you'd ever find, which is why it was particularly disturbing to see her as frightened as she was. She was pretty nervous around people (with the exception of kids), and she was hard to catch, difficult to lead, and would not tie to anything to save her life, which is, as I understand it, where her problems originated.

The story goes that a number of years ago Missy was standing tied to the hitch rail. A couple of horses tied next to her began to fight and frightened her so much that she pulled back in an

attempt to get away from them. Well, the rope she was tied with was old and rotten, and as she leaned back, it broke and she got loose. Now Missy had never been any trouble and had certainly never tried to pull back before. More than likely, had she been left alone, she would never have pulled back again. However, one of the wranglers working at the ranch decided to "teach her how to give to pressure" so that she would never break another lead rope.

The wrangler took old Missy, snubbed her to the hitch rail, and began to slap her in the face with the end of a lead rope. It didn't take long before Missy decided it might be a good idea to get away from that fellow, and so she pulled back. The good news was that neither the lead rope nor the halter broke when she pulled back. The bad news was that the hitch rail did. Once again, Missy had broken loose by pulling backwards.

The wrangler tied Missy to another hitch rail and continued to hit her in the face with a lead rope. Missy pulled back hard, this time breaking her halter and getting away. She was caught up, double haltered, and tied again. That time she broke her lead rope.

Over the next three months, the wrangler successfully taught Missy to pull back and break anything and everything she was tied to. From that point on, things went from bad to worse. Instead of hitting her in the face when she pulled back, people had taken to hitting her on the hindquarters. It didn't help; she was still breaking things.

The manager cemented a nine-inch post into the ground and tied her to that. After one time there, she refused to get close enough to allow herself to be tied to it again. They tied her to a fourteen-inch post that was part of a loading dock. After pulling back from that one time and breaking away, she never got close to it again, either. They had taken to tying big ropes around her middle and running them up through her halter before tying her with them. They hit her in the butt with pitchforks and chains and finally shot her with a pellet gun every time she pulled back. Year after year they kept trying to come up with something new to teach her not to pull back, and year after year she continued to pull back. After eleven long years one thing was clear . . . nothing they had done worked.

By the time I met Missy, she had pretty much had it with people. In fact, just the year before there had been talk of sending her to the killers, and she probably would have ended up there, too, had it not been for her one saving grace. She was great with kids. Even with all the trouble she'd had with adults, she still seemed to have a real soft spot for the kids who came to ride her. She had taught more kids how to ride than any other five horses on the ranch combined. I'm as sure as I can be that if it hadn't been for that, she'd have been sent down the road long ago.

Evidently, my reputation as a trainer who had worked with "problem" horses preceded me to the ranch, because as soon as I took over, one of the most-asked questions of me was, "How are you going to get Missy to stop pulling back?" To be honest, I didn't have a clue. One thing I knew for sure was that her days of being hit for not standing tied were over.

One of the first things I did when I began working at the ranch was get to know all the horses, and in particular, I got to know Missy. What I quickly found was that she was one of the sweetest mares I had ever come across, but her trust in humankind, particularly the taller sort, was nonexistent. My first priority was to somehow gain her trust back. In an attempt to gain some of that trust, I let her tell me what was going to be okay with her, and what wasn't, when we handled her.

She told us straight out that there were a few things that she would not tolerate. One was that we couldn't tie her in a tie stall in the barn. She didn't like to be saddled too quickly, it made her nervous. She didn't like people pulling on her lead rope, asking her to walk faster. That, in reality, was one of her cues to pull back. She didn't like to get too close to the loading dock; that made her nervous. She didn't like to be tied at all when standing at the hitch rails, or anywhere else for that matter—*If you tie me, I'll pull back. Period.* She also didn't like to stand next to certain horses. They made her nervous. She didn't like people coming up fast from behind or in front of her. That made her nervous. She didn't like to have reins or ropes swung around her face, shoulders, back, or hindquarters, for obvious reasons. So, there you go. Those were Missy's ground rules.

But the question remained. How would we get her to stop pulling back when tied? I gave the question a great deal of thought and, after several weeks of deliberation, finally came to a decision . . . we just wouldn't tie her. Not only would we not tie her, but we wouldn't do any of the other things she didn't like, either.

As you can imagine, this was somewhat bewildering for those who thought I would come up with some earth-shattering technique for teaching a horse how to stand tied. In fact, I believe there were those who figured I simply didn't want to deal with the problem and had chosen to avoid it. In reality, though, I figured that this might be one of those cases where the best way to fix a problem is to act like it doesn't exist. So, that's what we did.

From that day forward, we saddled Missy as slowly as was comfortable for her. We made sure that we didn't pull on her lead rope when we led her. When we took her out to the hitch rail, we draped her lead rope over the rail but never tied it. We made sure she never had to stand next to a horse that made her nervous, that no one ever rushed up in front of or behind her, and finally that no one ever swung a lead rope around her, if it could be helped. Now don't get me wrong. We weren't tiptoeing around her. We still went about our business, just as we would if she were any other horse on the place. It's just that, when it came to dealing exclusively with her, we made an effort not to do things that we felt would cause her a problem unnecessarily.

By working with her in such a way, I hoped that she would start to perceive us as being dependable for her, and even if she could never trust us completely, I hoped she would at least be a little more comfortable with her surroundings. Even at that, I don't mind telling you that it took a while before Missy began to come around. Months passed before we began to see a change in her. Slowly but surely, though, the change did come. Over time, things that had been very stressful for her weren't such a big deal anymore. People rushing behind or in front of her no longer got the same kind of panicked reaction. Tension on her lead rope while she was being led no longer caused her to pull back. She could stand to be saddled no matter how fast someone went around her, and most importantly, she could stand tied at the hitch rail.

We found that last little bit of information out quite by accident one day toward the end of the season. Every year we lost some of our help the last few weeks of the season, usually because we hired college students and they had to get back to school for the fall semester. Well, we had hired a young lady as a replacement for one of our summer staff who'd left, and she hadn't yet learned all of the horses in the string and so didn't know of Missy's past or her troubles. After Missy had come in from a trail ride, the new wrangler gathered her up, took her to the hitch rail, and tied her up like she would have any other horse. By the time someone noticed, Missy had been standing tied for over an hour and never once offered to pull back. It was, by far, a new record for Missy, who's longest period tied prior to that was about a minute-and-a-half. All that time we had been avoiding tying her, even after she had begun to settle into the routine, and she had been telling us that it wasn't really an issue for her anymore. From that day forward, Missy had no trouble standing tied.

I guess sometimes we get so tangled up in trying to find ways to teach our horses to do things or in finding training "techniques" to help us solve our horse's problems, that we forget to take the most important factor into consideration—the horse.

It seems to me that by giving our horses half a chance to tell us what's on their minds and genuinely listening to what they have to say, we can open the door to a whole new line of communication with them, one that perhaps wasn't even there before. By doing so, we allow ourselves the opportunity to get *all* the options on the table ... even the ones that our horses might be suggesting. This allows us to make a truly informed decision as to what course might be the correct one to take and limits the mistakes we might make in the long run.

When it gets right down to it, what I am talking about here is trust. Trusting our horses to do the right thing by us and doing the right thing by our horses. Of course, before our horses can really trust us, we must first prove to them that we can be fair in our decision-making. What better way is there to develop that fairness than to let our horse have his say from time to time? Not that we always have to go along with his idea, mind you. But, by the same token, he may not always be wrong, either.

Perhaps the best way to become a trusted leader for our horses is to first demonstrate that we aren't afraid to be a follower every once in a while. It's not a sin to let our horses tell us when some-thing is wrong or to let them make a decision from time to time. If it's a good decision, we can go with it. If it's a bad decision, we can be prepared to show them why it was a bad decision and what *we* can do to help them out of it. By doing so, we're not only avoiding a potential fight, but we are also showing our horses that we can be counted on to be fair in just about every situation.

Giving a horse that chance may be all it takes for him to begin to see you as his leader, especially in times when that is most important. After all, that just may be what being a leader is all about.

NOTES FOR HALF A CHANCE

When I wrote this chapter over ten years ago, I chose to focus on two horses who, when given a half a chance, showed just how good a horse they really were. The two I spoke about here weren't the only horses I'd run into up to that point who were able to make such a change when treated a little differently than they had been in the past. They were just the two that sort of stuck out in my mind at the time.

As I read through the chapter in preparation for making these notes, it struck me that if I were to write the same chapter today just how many more examples I would have to choose from. With-out even giving the subject too much serious thought, my mem-ory nearly becomes flooded with horses we've worked with in the past ten years that just needed half a chance to show the kind of wonderful animal that was hiding under that worried, troubled or defensive exterior.

It got me to thinking that if there were any one chapter in this book that really illustrates the horse's need to follow a leader they can trust, it would be this one. Truly, as was demonstrated by Bud and Missy's stories, when given half a chance and a little direction that makes sense to them, the vast majority of horses out there will do what they can to find a way to get along.

Will it Work?

It's funny, the things that go through a person's mind when he's closing the door on one part of his life and getting ready to walk through another. Those were my thoughts as I looked at the pile of tack sitting on the floor of the 110-year-old barn that had been my office and home away from home. For the past hour, I'd been going through the barn gathering everything that belonged to me. Piece by piece, I had taken my things from the places they'd occupied for years and had set them near the door where I would soon load it all into my pickup and haul it away.

In that pile were the tools of my trade: saddles and saddle pads, halters, lead ropes, headstalls, leather reins, a couple sets of long driving lines, my duster and slicker, chaps, gloves, shoeing and leather tools, lariats, and cotton ropes of all lengths and sizes. As I placed the last lead rope over the seat of one of my saddles, I stepped back and gazed at the pile, shaking my head at the recent turn of events.

For over eight years, I'd been working in one capacity or another at this guest ranch. I started as a sort of consultant on operations safety, then moved into the position of full-time trainer. A year later I was promoted to ranch foreman and, a year after that, had moved my family from our place just outside town to a house on the ranch. We had lived on the ranch just over four years, but our time there had recently come to an abrupt end. The day after the summer season was over, I was called into a meeting with the new owners and promptly fired. The new owners—devout Christians—told me that they felt I had not attended enough of the Christian activities they provided for the employees and guests of the ranch during the summer. Even though I had provided them with what they called a "top-of-the-line, first-class horse program," I could no longer be a part of the ranch "family." We had been given sixty days to vacate the premises.

As I walked through the barn, checking one last time to make sure I had everything, my mind drifted back to my very first days on the place. The owner at that time had hired me to help bring the ranch horses and the program itself up to snuff. The ranch had had a number of horse-related accidents, and he wanted to make the program safer while improving the overall quality of the product he provided to his guests. The owner knew that I had previously run a couple of other horse programs at other ranches and that the horses on those places became more responsive for the guests and that safety had improved to the point that the ranches were accident-free. That was the type of program he was looking for and one he hoped I could help him develop.

The biggest asset I felt I brought to the situation was my experience with the old man all those years ago. Because of the time I'd spent with him, I knew how easy things on a horse operation could be. Many livery or "dude" operations go at what they do with very little consideration for the horse. Basically, these places have a "slap a saddle on 'em and get 'em out of here" mentality. The horses wind up being little more than a means to an end, and very often it's the horses that protest the loudest about the arrangement by becoming hard to catch, running off with riders, bucking people off, rubbing people off on trees, spooking at inopportune times, or just being contrary in general. However, I had always felt that a good way to avoid all that might be to treat the horses with quiet consistency and to give them trust, dignity, and respect, just as the old man had done with his horses. If we could do that, perhaps things would be different, even in a dude operation.

First we needed to find the right kind of people to help run the place. They needed to be people with horse experience, but they also needed to be people with the right attitude. We needed people who would give the horse the benefit of the doubt in most situations and who would think through a problem with a horse instead of just reacting to it. We wanted people who could think on their feet but who had soft hands and good hearts. In short, they needed to be people who would always put the horses first. Some of the best of them came back to work at the ranch year after year and are now out working with horses on their own.

Once the right people were hired, it was time to give the place itself a face-lift. We built a new tack room and office, a new foaling stall, new four-rail wooden fences all over the ranch, extra corrals, two new round pens, and a massive riding arena. New hitch rails were put in under the shade of towering pines so the horses that weren't out on rides during the day were always out of the sun and rain. Finally, all the employees knew that the ranch was to remain spotless at all times. Manure would be picked up as soon as it hit the ground, the barn floor would be swept at least three times a day, and the entire area, including the driveway and all riding trails within sight of it, would be raked at least once per day.

Keeping the fences in good repair and keeping the place clean gave the employees a sense of pride that they didn't want to let go of. It also helped them keep their enthusiasm for their day-to-day duties on the ranch. This pride was not only evident throughout the summer but was passed down from one crew to the next and from one year to the next.

With the crew hired and the place itself in order, it was finally time to start working with the horses. One of the very first things we did was fit the horses with their own tack. You see, in the past when a guest would sign up to ride, the wrangler would size up the guest the night before and assign the guest to a particular saddle. That saddle was placed on whatever horse the wranglers happened to catch the next day. As a result, the horses were constantly wearing saddles that didn't fit them and, in turn, were constantly sore backed.

We systematically placed each saddle on each horse until we found the saddle that best fit the horse. Once we found a saddle that fit, it became part of that horse's individual tack. We also fit each horse with a bridle. In the saddle room, each horse had a peg for its saddle, and the pegs were in alphabetical order according to each horse's name. In the bridle room, the bridles were also hung in alphabetical order, which made them easy to find and eliminated mix-ups.

Once we had all the horses fit for tack, we focused on physical problems. Dr. Dave Siemans, the equine chiropractor whom I had worked with for many years, adjusted the horses that had back, neck, hip, or shoulder problems. We had the horses vetted and dewormed and had their teeth floated. We also changed hay suppliers to get a hay rich in protein, carbohydrates, and other nutrients. And we went from feeding a straight, rolled-oat grain with little nutritional value to a supplement designed specifically for our horses' needs. With these changes, we began to see a noticeable difference in them. They began putting on weight and could actually keep it on. The horses had more energy and seemed more willing to work.

Then we switched our focus to the horses' feet. Most of the horses at the ranch had become hard to shoe. Many had back problems due to ill-fitting tack. Because their backs hurt, they had hip and shoulder problems. Because they had back and shoulder problems, they began to cramp up when the farrier was working on them. Due to the pain they were in, they would often take their foot away during shoeing.

The other problem was the farrier whom the ranch had used. This fellow was a very good farrier, but he was short on finesse and patience. A horse didn't take his foot away very many times before it got a kick in the belly or a whack with the rasp. The horses were scared when the farrier came around, and problems often began before he even got started.

169

We found a new farrier who was not only good at his job but was also good with the horses. He would take as much time as he needed to work around the horses without fighting with them. He made sure that the shoes fit and that the horses were always in balance with themselves when he was finished. With the soreness gone and a more patient farrier, the majority of our shoeing problems just melted away.

We worked quietly with any horses that still had problems picking up or holding up their feet for the farrier. Sometimes we spent days, or even weeks, doing nothing with a horse but picking up its feet just a little bit at a time. For a couple of horses, we had to start by picking the foot up only an inch or so off the ground, building on that until we could pick it all the way up and place it in the position the farrier required. With these horses, we took as much time as they needed to teach them how to hold their feet and wouldn't allow the farrier to work with them until we were sure they were ready—we refused to set the horse up to fail.

With the majority of the "incidental" issues out of the way, it was finally time to get down to the business of training and retraining the horses for the job that we would be expecting of them. As I said, the goal of the owner, as well as our goal, was to have horses that were consistently responsive and willing through the entire summer season. So, with that, it was time for myself, the wranglers, and the horses to begin to develop the relationships that would allow the whole thing to come together.

The emphasis was on "soft." No matter what else happened, the wranglers were to stay soft while riding the horses. Soft hands, soft seat, and soft legs. There was to be absolutely no hitting, kicking, slapping, or yelling at any time for any reason. The penalty for doing such things was to be placed on a two-day suspension. A second offense would lead to termination. Neither penalty was ever needed.

At times it wasn't easy to stay quiet with the horses because so many of them had been "used up" over the years, dulled to any form of cue. However, we remained consistent in our focus and the horses responded.

The wranglers were instructed to ride the horses with the softest cues possible, often using nothing more than a light squeeze to get forward movement and a shift of weight in the saddle, along with light pressure on the reins, for a stop. They were also instructed to look for, find, and then release their cues at the slightest try from the horse—something they all became very adept at doing. With everyone riding in the same manner from one day to the next, all the horses began to respond within a few weeks. Before we knew it, all of our horses, including the very old ones that had been in the program for years and years, became responsive to the lightest of cues.

We'd taught our horses to be responsive to these light cues, but a question remained. How could we keep them that way, particularly with the hundreds of different people who would be riding each horse over the summer? The answer was simple. Everyone needed to remain consistent. So, instead of expecting our horses to respond to the conflicting cues that each new rider was bound to give, we taught each rider how to communicate with our horses.

Each week when a new batch of guests arrived at the ranch, we held an orientation in the riding arena. During this orientation, we explained how our horses were trained and what was expected of them as a rider of one of our horses. We gave them a demonstration in the saddle of proper seat and hand position, so they could keep their balance. We showed them the cues for walk, stop, trot, lope, and turn, using a horse right out of the string. Once we had demonstrated how our horses worked, we got everyone on horseback in the arena and helped them to practice giving the cues, allowing the horse to respond, and releasing the cues so that the horse would remain responsive.

Of note is the fact that after the orientation was over, people not only signed up for trail rides, but a great number of folks also signed up for the riding lessons we provided. Few of them had experienced horses as responsive and quiet as ours, and they wanted to learn more about how we got them that way and how we could help them improve their own riding skills. After the first couple of years, our instructional program had become even more popular than the trail rides we offered. That's really saying something when you realize that most of our trail rides went through the heart of Rocky Mountain National Park.

Our goal had been to produce one of the finest horse programs around, but for me, there was a larger, more important goal—to gain a mutual trust between us and our horses. I figured that if we had mutual trust, our horses would *want* to perform the job we were asking of them, instead of feeling like they had no other option. I wanted them to be willing partners in the job and I needed to make it as easy on them to perform their job as I could. That meant putting the horses in the right frame of mind so they wouldn't feel the need to fight with us. By teaching the horses how to be soft, we were able to put them in the right frame of mind. By teaching our guests how to be soft, we were able to keep the horses in that frame of mind.

Even at that, there was still more to the picture. I felt right along that in order for the thing to be truly successful, we needed to be even more consistent. Up to this point, we'd relied primarily on "surface" things to accomplish our goals. Don't get me wrong, I consider everything that we'd done very important, but I also felt that those things were based primarily on the horses learning or relearning certain things. In order for it all to come together, we needed to tap into the "feel" of the overall operation.

It has been my experience that every horse place, whether it be a boarding operation, training facility, dude ranch, or just someone's backyard, will have a certain feel to it. It's in the atmosphere of the place itself, and usually I can feel it as soon as I step out of the pickup. The old man's place, for instance, had a quiet feeling of togetherness between the horses and people that were there. It was a feeling that everyone was on the same page and that they were all there to help one another. In contrast, I've been to barns where the tension between horses and people, or even between people and people, was so thick you could cut it with a knife.

I believe there are a number of factors that cause a place to have a certain feel, but the greatest factor has to be the people who operate and use the place. Ultimately, it is what they do and how they do it that forms the foundation of the atmosphere created there.

The feel of a place, in my opinion, has a great deal to do with how horses respond to us when we're working with them. For instance, in a place with a quiet feeling of togetherness, like the atmosphere created by the old man, the horses are almost always willing and easy to get along with. On the other hand, horses at a place where the tension and stress level is through the roof respond in kind, with high anxiety and a lot of pent-up stress that seems unmanageable at times.

When I first started at the ranch, I would have had to say that our operation was somewhere between the two. It wasn't a real comfortable place to be, but it wasn't unbearable either. So, one of my priorities was to see if we couldn't perhaps create a better atmosphere for both our horses and us.

We'd already gotten a jump on this with the people we'd hired. They were all good horse people and lacked the large egos that often create problems. They were all very conscientious workers and became fast friends almost immediately. Each was willing to help the other whenever help was needed, and there was a sense of kinship between them that, in many cases, lasts to this day. Because our staff was so good, it made the rest of the process very easy.

I feel like one of the biggest things that helped create the positive atmosphere at the old man's place was the fact that he seldom, if ever, made a big deal out of anything. He never yelled at anyone that I know of, and he never fought with his horses. As a result, there was an air about him that said that even if something bad did happen on the place, everything would be okay anyway. He made it easy for his horses to look to him as someone who could be counted on and trusted when things went bad. That was the feeling we wanted to create at the ranch. It was mostly already in place, due to the excellent staff. The rest would come over time and would manifest itself in the way we handled the day-to-day situations that came up.

During the months and years that followed, we began to achieve the feeling of trust and confidence with our horses that we'd been looking for. Several factors helped us. The first was that we were willing to stand up for our horses when they needed it. If a guest was getting heavy-handed with one of our horses, we stopped the behavior immediately. Sometimes it didn't make the guest real happy, but the horse appreciated it.

The second factor was that we let our horses have their say and tried to listen to them. Several times we had horses tell us when they were having trouble carrying a rider because they were sore or not feeling well. In those cases, when a horse began to act "different," we pulled the horse from service, had it looked at by the vet, chiropractor, or farrier, fixed the problem, and put the horse back in service. Each time we did this with a horse, its performance and attitude improved greatly.

We weren't afraid to let a horse have his or her say in other situations, either. For instance, a few weeks into the season, one of our mares would suddenly stop on the trail, turn around, and head for home, for no apparent reason. Our first thought was that something was physically wrong with her. We had her thoroughly checked over, but no one could find anything wrong with her, so we put her back in service. Again she began to head for home, and again we had her checked out. After getting her second clean bill of health, we decided that she was trying to tell us that she just wanted to go home.

We decided that the best way to cure her was to let her have her way and then show her that her idea wasn't the best option. Instead of fighting with her out on the trail, we had a wrangler ride her with instructions to bring her back to the barn at a lope the next time she tried to turn around and come home. Back at the barn, he would immediately take the mare into the arena and ask her to lope first one direction, then the other, for ten minutes or so. After that, he would ask her to head back out on the trail at a walk. If the mare tried to turn around, he was to let her and then repeat the process.

The next time it happened, the wrangler worked with the mare for quite a while in that fashion. In fact, the ride that she'd originally gone out on had returned to the barn while she was still working. Shortly after the other horses returned, however, it suddenly came to her that she was doing a whole lot more work than she really needed to. After heading out on the trail and walking quietly to a point past where she had turned around originally, the wrangler dismounted and walked the mare back to the barn. Even in a situation like this, we still treated her with the respect and dignity that she deserved. She never did turn around on the trail again.

The third thing we did that I believe helped achieve the atmosphere we wanted was to make it clear to our horses that we were willing to draw the line with them when we needed to. We were willing to give them the benefit of the doubt, listen to what they had to say, and treat them with the respect due to them, but we also expected the same from them in return. We let them know that we needed them to have manners on the trails, in the arena, and any other time they were being handled. Safety was still a priority, and the best way to stay safe was to make sure the horses knew the ground rules.

Basically these rules consisted of: no running people over while being led; no kicking at people or other horses in the barn or while they were being tacked up; standing quietly to be haltered, bridled, and saddled; and no kicking at other horses on the trails or when performing lessons in the arena. They were also expected to walk to the barn from the hitch rail to get their lunch or when it was time to be untacked.

It didn't take long to find that enforcing these rules in a non-violent, low-impact way was pretty easy and very effective. A horse that offered to ran someone over while being led was taken back to the point of origin and tied back up. This seldom happened, but when it did it was usually on the way to the barn at the end of the day. The horse that had been in a hurry to be untacked ended up being the last one standing with a saddle on his back. The next day, the horse would usually walk very politely to the barn.

In the case where a horse might get a little kicky in the barn, one of the wranglers would remove him from the barn, and he wouldn't get to finish his meal. The kicking usually stopped pretty quickly. Horses that didn't stand to be tacked up were tied outside until the entire herd had eaten and been tacked up. Only then would they be saddled.

A horse that got a little kicky on the trail or in the arena was first looked at by the vet, chiropractor, or farrier to make sure they were physically fit to be working. If there was a problem, which was the case nine times out of ten, we had them worked on. If it wasn't a soreness issue, we began looking at other causes, such as the horse behind them being their dire enemy in the pasture. More times than not, just moving the horses around from one spot to another within the line was enough to stop the problem.

Now, one of the most interesting things we did with our horses was teach them how to walk on their own to the barn at lunch time. Once taught, we also used it at the end of the day when the horses were to be untacked. We came up with this idea shortly after I'd taken over. During the day, we fed our horses three different times: once in the morning in the barn; once at lunch time in the barn; and once at the end of the day, out in the pasture. The two feedings in the barn consisted of a grain-type supplement, the feeding in the pasture was a grass hay.

When we first started, we led the horses two at a time from the hitch rail nearly sixty feet to the barn, where we let them in to get their lunch. This was very time consuming and took nearly the entire crew to accomplish. A year or two later, one of the wranglers came up with the idea to let the horses walk to the barn on their own. By doing this, we would only need two people to feed lunch to the entire herd, one to let the horses loose from the hitch rails and one to catch them at the door of the barn and lead them into a waiting stall.

The problem was how to teach the horses to *walk* to the barn on their own. By the time lunch came around, the horses were not only hungry, but they knew they were going to get grain, making their desire to run to the barn just that much stronger. With no one there to stop them from running, why should they walk? We would not only be asking them to do something that they had never done before, we would also be asking them to fight a natural urge to get to their food just as quickly as possible.

We gave the situation a little thought and came up with an idea. In order to stick with our goal of helping the horses learn things, instead of demanding that they learn them, we needed to show them what was expected. To that end, when we started to teach the process to the herd, our plan was to do so by walking the first three or four horses to the barn, just as we had in the past. We would then begin to turn the others lose, one horse at a time. Any horse that walked to the barn would be allowed to go in and get his lunch. Any horse that went faster than a walk would be caught at the door of the barn and tied up outside. That would be the only deterrent we would use.

After the first three or four horses were led in, the next several all trotted or loped and were caught and tied up. The next horse, an old gelding that never ran anywhere, took his time getting to the barn. He was allowed to go in. The next horse trotted and was tied up. The

horse after him, however, had been paying attention and walked all the way to the barn, and he, too, was allowed inside. Of the fifty or so head that we turned loose that day, only about a third of them made it into the barn. When we turned them loose the next day, almost half made it in. The day after that, a little over half of them made it, and by the fifth day, nearly all were walking to the barn. In less than a week's time, all fifty head had learned that they were on the honor system and the only way to get lunch was to mind their manners.

The thing that's intriguing isn't so much that we were able to accomplish our goal without using some high-tech training technique or the fact that we never had to get physical with any of the horses. No, the most interesting thing to me is that it was clear that the horses that were tied up for running watched very closely what was going on with the others. They could see that some horses were getting in and some weren't. Within a short period of time, they all figured out what *they* needed to do to be one of those that would get in. They had sorted it out in their own minds, then made a decision as to what would be best for them in the long run. Just like that, they had learned right from wrong with very little intervention from us.

I guess if I had to put what we were trying to do with all of this into words, I would say that we were simply trying to find a way to get along with our horses so that we didn't have to be constantly bossing them around. In doing so, we were looking for a way to form a partnership, not only between us and our horses, but also between our horses and whatever guest happened to be riding them. It was a pretty tall order, but I truly believe we may have gotten as close as anyone might.

When it was all said and done, we had accomplished our goal of having responsive horses that worked willingly, day-in and day-out, from the end of May until the middle of September, not just for one season, but for several years straight. To top it off, each horse averaged around 150 different riders of all sizes, shapes, and skill levels each summer. Even with that many people riding them, each horse still remained just as responsive for the last person who rode in September as they had been for the first one in May.

I should also point out here that our horses, even though they were considered "dude" horses, were actually asked to do much more than simply packing people nose-to-tail up and down mountain trails. On top of the regular trail rides that we did at a walk for inexperienced riders, we also did guided intermediate and advanced rides, where guests could ride in a controlled trot and lope for a portion of their trip. We did a number of riding lessons for people who had never been close to a horse before, as well as for folks who not only owned, but also competed with their own horses back home. We even taught some first- and second-level dressage folks how to ride the western performance horses that we had trained right there on the ranch. These folks would be doing reinless stops from the lope, rollbacks without having to use the leg, and flawless transitions by an almost imperceivable shift of their weight in the saddle. They would take these same horses out of the arena and go on a two-hour trail ride, and the horses never missed a step.

While our horses remained willing and responsive from one year to the next and from one rider to the next, we also found that by having gained their trust, we were getting some other positive behaviors from them as a bonus. For instance, we had a couple of horses come to us that were extremely "slicker shy." We thought about teaching them how to accept the sight and sound of a slicker by sacking them out with it, but on second thought we just decided to let it pass for a while until the horses got used to the place and the people around them. After being in the program for a while, we could see that these horses were beginning to gain some trust and become comfortable with our place and the people. At that time, we decided to introduce the slicker to them. Much to our surprise, after an initial sideways look at the unfolded slicker, the horses accepted it as if it had never been a big deal at all.

The same thing happened with a couple of horses that had come to us with a fear of crossing water. Once they gained trust in what we were all about, we took them down to our shallow pond, and after giving them just a few minutes to look at it, they often walked in even without so much as a small argument. We had horses with a history of being hard to catch that, over time, would suddenly be okay with letting people walk up to them, and still others that in the past had refused to load into a trailer but now would walk right in. I know, it sounds too easy, but it was easy. To be honest, it was often so easy that when something like this happened, it would surprise everyone involved. Quite frankly, it surprised me, too.

Before anyone gets the wrong idea, I guess I should point out that I'm not saying that gaining our horse's trust takes the place of good, sound training. I'm not saying that at all. What I am saying is that we definitely saw a marked increase in the willingness of the horses to accept whatever it was we were presenting to them at any given time. As a result, it didn't matter much what kind of technique or method we used for the training itself, as long as we went at the whole thing with the right attitude.

Our attitude was that we were going to be consistent, we weren't going to hurt our horses, and we didn't care how long it took for them to understand what we were trying to show them. The funny thing was that the more we came at the horses with an attitude of "I don't care how long this takes," the quicker everything seemed to go. This, coupled with the fact that we had already earned their trust by the way we'd treated them, usually made even the most difficult of training tasks seem not quite so difficult. Because the horses trusted our judgment, it was easier for them to accept what we were showing them during that training, and as a result, we had fewer issues or "attitudes" to work through first.

I'm not going to try to kid anyone here. What we did at the ranch took a great deal of time, commitment, and effort. The only way the whole thing worked on such a large scale was for everyone to be on the same page and have the same goal in mind at all times. Because of our commitment to and our consistency with our horses (and with each other, for that matter), I believe we were able to supply the horses with the dependability they needed in their day-to-day activities, thus making those activities as low-stress as possible. This dependability translated into a pretty unshakable trust between us and our horses that was evident in the performance they gave us each day. Because we had proven ourselves in their eyes to be individuals who could be trusted, it was easy for them to start looking to us as the leaders who they could—and would—*choose* to follow, instead of leaders who forced them to follow.

Since leaving the ranch, I've headed out on the road, performing training clinics and seminars all over the world. One thing I've found during my travels is that whenever people ask me questions about horses, those questions fit into one of two categories. The first is sort of, "What can I do to get my horse to respond to me better?" In other words, what technique can I use to accomplish the goal? The second is, "How can I make my relationship with my horse better so that he will *want* to work for me?"

In general, it seems that the people who ask the first kind of question are looking for surface fixes and aren't really concerned about what is going on inside the horse. They aren't necessarily concerned about how the horse perceives the situation, but are more concerned about getting what they consider to be the proper response from the horse. Unfortunately, training without feeling will usually only result in a sort of mechanical response from the horse. Because there is no feel behind either the cue that is given or the response given in return, the response itself will seldom be consistent. These folks have usually already discovered that fact, but they don't quite understand that the way they've worked with their horse is the cause of the inconsistent behavior they experience. They have relied so much on "cues" that the feel is nearly gone between themselves and their horse.

On the other hand, the folks who ask the second type of question are looking for something more. They're the ones searching for the connection between themselves and their horses that will allow everything else to happen. These folks, in my opinion, are the ones who will get the "cueless" transitions and the sliding stops and the flawless spins on a consistent basis because they aren't relying on cues ... they're relying on feel, the feeling between themselves and their horses.

However, it seems to me that before they can achieve that feel between themselves and their horses, they must first have some kind of relationship with the horse that is based on trust. To that end, it has been my experience that the best way to gain that trust is to simply be as consistently low-key as possible in handling our horses from day to day. Of course, that doesn't mean giving the horse the run of the place, but by the same token, it does mean presenting things to our horses in a way that's easy for them to understand and not losing our temper with them if they have trouble understanding.

I had a fellow bring me a horse that he was having trouble getting to canter. This was a gaited horse that presumably had been very well trained and had, near as we could tell, over twenty different gaits. He moved his feet in so many different ways while he was going forward that it was often difficult to tell one gait from the next or even one speed in the same gait from another. This was a relatively new horse for the man—he had only owned him for about six months—but already things were going downhill between the two of them. Because the man was having trouble getting the lope, he had used increasingly heavy cues and had finally taken to wearing spurs. Nothing had worked.

By the time I had the opportunity to work with them, the horse was extremely defensive and the man was getting short tempered. It was clear as soon as the man mounted up that there was very little trust between them. In fact, there was a sense that they were working against each other, rather than working together. They made only a lap or two around the arena, with the man kicking and slapping the horse with the reins, and the horse pinning his ears and crow hopping nearly the entire way, before I asked if I could ride the horse. The man quickly, with a sigh of relief, agreed.

It took about a half a lap for me to see why it was so frustrating for the owner to ride this horse. What I found was that the gelding acted like a high-performance sports car with a slipping transmission. Any little shift of weight in the saddle was enough for the horse to respond with a shift of speed. Even the slightest leg cue gave me a change of gait, but it was a very quick succession of changes, none of which I was actually asking for. His responsiveness to the rider was amazing, but I'm sure it was frustrating to him to feel that his attempts to do what he thought was right kept being met with more pressure and continual reprimands.

I let the horse travel for a lap or two, trying to get a feel for what he was all about, and then asked him for a lope by giving him just a little squeeze with my heels. The only response I received was a faster version of whatever gait he was in at the time. The longer I rode and the more cues I gave, the more I began to notice that everything I did, and I mean everything, meant one thing to me and something completely different to him.

I might have thought that a shift of my weight coupled with a little leg was supposed to mean that he should go from one gait to the next. To him it meant he was only supposed to increase speeds within the gait. It began to dawn on me that we shouldn't try to show him how to respond to us; instead we should concentrate on how we were supposed to respond to him. He already knew what he was supposed to do; we just didn't know how to ask properly.

So, with that, we backed way off and went at the entire thing differently. Instead of applying a cue and expecting to get a certain response, we would apply a cue and take whatever response we got. By working this way, we could let the horse tell us what a particular cue meant to him, thereby effectively eliminating the guesswork for both him and us. Within about thirty minutes, we had distinguished the difference between the cues for an increase in speed in any particular gait, a change of foot pattern within the gait, and a change from one gait to the next. Most of these cues were nothing more than a shift of weight in the saddle and the lifting of a rein or reins—far less than anything either the owner or I had been giving initially.

Once the meaning of the cues had been established for all involved, the tasks that we were looking for began to come much easier. After forty-five minutes of practicing the cues and paying attention to the responses to make absolutely sure we were on the same page, we asked for the lope using the cue we believed would mean "lope" to the horse. This cue was nothing more than a raising of the reins and a quiet kissing sound.

Just like that, the horse drifted up into one of the prettiest canters that anyone could hope for. No tail flick, no pinned ears, and no crow hopping, just a nice quiet transition in response to a nice quiet cue. Less than fifteen minutes after getting that first transition, we were able to lighten the cues to the point where we didn't even have to make the kissing sound anymore. A gentle lifting of the reins would do the trick. A few minutes after that, even the lifting of the reins lessened. We had gone from lifting the reins about eight inches, to lifting them less than three inches, and finally it was down to about half an inch. All less than an hour-and-a-half after we had started.

It turns out that all we had to do to accomplish our goal was let the horse tell us what we needed to be doing. He already knew what it would take, he just needed the opportunity to show us. In this case, we simply needed to allow ourselves to follow before we could step up and lead.

Over the years I have noticed a very distinct difference between horses that choose to see us as leaders and those that have been forced to follow. The difference is palpable. Every horse I've been involved with that truly trusted its owner was always willing to bend over backwards to do the right thing. The horse was always there for the owner when it was needed the most and would seldom, if ever, quit. Horses that have been forced into submission, on the other hand, bend just enough to get the task accomplished, but no more. If given the chance, the horse has no qualms about quitting when the owner needs it most.

In the end, I guess the only way a horse is going to decide to choose us as its leader is if we can show the horse that we can be dependable. How we choose to accomplish that is up to us. Whether the horse chooses to choose us is strictly up to it.

NOTES FOR WILL IT WORK

Looking back, one of the things in this chapter that I almost wish I hadn't mentioned was how the Christian owners of the guest ranch I was working at fired me because I wasn't attending enough of the Christian activities they had implemented since they bought and took the ranch over. I say I almost wish I hadn't mentioned it because I have since received numerous letters and emails, along with folks at clinics coming up and telling me how sorry they were that Christians would do such a thing.

I would like to take this opportunity to emphasize that I completely understand why the folks at the ranch did what they did, and that I don't hold it against them. Hopefully, nobody else will either. Leaving the ranch, while very difficult at the time, opened up a number of amazing and very positive doors for me that I probably would have never had the chance to explore if I were still there. I prefer to focus on that aspect of the situation rather than any negative that may have come from it.

On the complete opposite end of the spectrum is something else I mentioned in this chapter that I was hoping folks would take to heart, but from some of the feedback I've gotten, it seems many people almost completely overlooked. That was the point I made regarding the idea that when working toward developing a leadership role with a horse, how important it is to make sure the horse understands boundaries, as well as the difference between what we might see as positive behavior from them as opposed to negative behavior.

I think sometimes folks get so focused on wanting to have a harmonious relationship with their horse, they forget that horses, just like people, need to understand how to do their job properly in order to be comfortable doing it. It's difficult for a horse to feel comfortable when there are no boundaries or limitations put on their behavior. In a herd situation, boundaries are one of the first things horses learn from other horses, followed closely by learning how to act as a productive member of the herd through limitations on their behavior. I think it's important to remember that good horsemanship, just like life itself, is all about keeping things in balance. There can't be comfort without a little discomfort, and there can't be balance unless things become a little unbalanced from time to time. When we can learn to embrace those times when things aren't going as well as we would like, and then find ways to deal with them in a productive manner, that's when I believe horses can begin to look to us as a leader they can trust.

The Connection

The woman had called a few days earlier and asked if I'd come and have a look at her horse. For the past few months, she'd been noticing that her gelding, a five-year-old she'd owned for three years, had become real cranky whenever she asked anything of him. Even her slightest requests were being met with head shakes, foot stomps, and constant tail wringing. He was even becoming hard to catch. Because the behavior was getting progressively worse as the days went on, she had decided to try to get a handle on it before it was completely out of control.

As I pulled into the driveway, I could see the woman leading the gelding from a paddock behind the house up to a small hitch rail near a fairly new round pen a few yards away. The gelding, a nice-looking palomino, was walking quietly some two feet behind the woman, head down, eyes soft, with a very relaxed look about him. Suddenly, for no reason that I could see, the woman turned and began vigorously shaking the horse's lead rope. The lead had a large, metal bull snap attached to the horse's rope halter, and each time she shook the lead, that snap would swing up and hit the horse on the bottom of his jaw. His head popped up, his eyes widened, his body stiffened, and he began backing at a fast pace.

He backed probably six or eight feet before the woman stopped shaking the rope, but the heavy bull snap was still moving and it hit him one more time in the jaw. That caused the horse to back another two or three feet before he stopped. His head remained high and his eyes were wide, but without hesitating, the woman turned and walked forward again. The horse followed, but this time he was much more alert and his steps were tentative.

They had gone only about ten feet when I saw the first sign of what the woman had talked about when she'd phoned me. The horse suddenly shook his head and wrung his tail. The woman didn't seem to notice, however, and continued over to the hitch rail. She tied the gelding and turned to meet me as I made my way over to the two of them.

We stood and visited for a few minutes as she explained in more detail what she had been doing with the horse over the past three years. She had been going to some clinics with him, where she'd learned many ground-work techniques, as well as some ways to get more impulsion in the saddle. She told me that she'd been using the techniques she had learned religiously, and at first everything seemed to be going just fine. However, as time went on, she began to notice "sour" behavior in her horse each time she used one of the techniques. She was especially concerned about the fact that he was getting increasingly unhappy with the ground work she did with him. Because the importance of "proper" ground work had been stressed at the clinics and because it was supposed to be tied to gaining the horse's respect, she was becoming concerned that her horse's sour attitude was a sign that she was doing something wrong.

I asked her to show me what she had been doing with the horse and what, exactly, the behavior was that she was concerned about. She happily agreed, went over and untied the gelding from the hitch rail, and began leading him to the round pen. They had only gone a few feet when she turned and began shaking her lead rope. The horse, head high, immediately began backing.

"Can I ask why you did that?" I inquired, when she had stopped shaking the lead.

"Did what?" she asked, as the horse shook his head.

"Shook the lead rope like that."

"Oh," she nodded, "he was crowding me and so any time he does that I'm supposed to back him off by doing this."

She shook the lead rope to demonstrate, and the horse responded by raising his head and backing a few feet.

"That's okay," I told her. "You don't have to show me."

"Is there something wrong with backing him off like that?" she asked.

The horse had quietly begun to lower his head as she was talking, but she shook the lead rope again, lightly. The bull snap flipped up, tapping the horse on the jaw, and he raised his head and took a step back.

"Not necessarily," I shrugged. "How close to you does he have to be before you feel like he's crowding you?"

"Oh, I don't know," she turned and looked at the horse. "It varies, I guess. Sometimes I don't mind it when he's close, other times I'd rather have him a little farther away."

"I see," I nodded. "So, how does he know the difference between when it's all right to come close and when it's not?"

"When I shake the lead rope, he's too close," she said. "That's how he knows."

"So, basically, you allow him to make the mistake, then you make the correction?" I questioned.

"I guess you could say that," she replied.

"Do you have to make a lot of these corrections?"

The horse began to slowly drop his head, as though he was relaxing. The woman gently shook the lead rope as she gave the question a little thought. The horse's head popped back up, he stomped his foot, and wrung his tail.

"I wouldn't say I have to make a lot of corrections," she said, as she slowly shook her head.

"I see," I nodded. "Well, why don't we go on in the round pen so you can show me the problems that you're having?"

With that, we headed over to the round pen and I opened the gate for them so they could go through ahead of me. The woman stopped just short of the gate, however, pointed toward the opening, and began to lightly swing her rope at the horse's hindquarters. The horse blew hard through his nose, wrung his tail, then walked through the gate and into the round pen.

"Why did you do that?" I asked.

"Do what?" she replied, as the horse hit the end of the lead rope, which caused him to turn all the way back around and face her.

"Why did you send him through in front of you?"

"Because I want him to know who's in control here." She had not yet moved into the pen with the horse, which gave the appearance that she may have wanted him to come back out. He hesitated a few seconds and slowly stepped toward her. She responded by shaking the lead rope.

"He should just go wherever I tell him to go. That way he knows who's in charge."

The horse shook his head, wrung his tail, and stomped his right front foot. She shook the lead rope again, backing him farther into the pen. This time she followed him through the gate, turned, and led him out to the middle of the pen. I went in and closed the gate behind me.

"Okay," she said. "What would you like to see first?"

"I guess we should just start at the beginning," I told her. "Why don't you just go about your business with him like you normally would?"

She nodded, pointed off to her left, and began swinging the lead rope at the horse's hip. He went out to the end of the twelve-foot lead and moved into a trot, but not before shaking his head and wringing his tail. The woman stood as the horse circled around her. He made only two laps before she gave the rope a little tug, to which he responded by turning in her direction and moving toward her. She shook the rope, backing him away from her. Another head shake. She let him stand for a few seconds, then pointed to the right and repeated the entire process. Again, after a couple of laps, she tugged on the rope and he tried to come to her, but she shook the rope and kept him away. He wrung his tail and shook his head.

"See," she said. "That's what he does."

"I see," I nodded. "What else can you show me?"

"He really has trouble yielding his hindquarters," she said, moving to his back end and touching him lightly on his hip with her hand. He immediately began to step over, away from her, but wrung his tail the entire time.

"See what I mean? He seems really agitated by this."

She went to his front end and began shaking both forefingers at his neck, as if they were pistols.

"He's not much better with yielding his front end either," she said, continuing to shake her fingers and move into the horse as he stepped away from her. Again he wrung his tail and this time added a pretty vigorous head shake.

"See what I mean?"

"How often do you ask him to do these things?" I asked.

"I don't know," she replied. "Just about every time I work with him, I guess. I've been trying to get him to do them without the attitude, but he's been getting worse instead of better."

She went on to show me a number of other ground-work exercises she'd taught the horse, each one receiving a similar response from him. For the most part, the gelding would perform whatever task she asked of him, but always with some sort of mild protest.

From my perspective, it was pretty clear that the gelding had just about had it with all of these little things that he was being asked to do. Not that he wasn't doing them, because he was. It was just that many of the tasks didn't seem to have any point behind them. He couldn't understand why he was continually being asked to do things that he not only knew how to do, but that didn't seem to have any purpose.

For instance, why was he being asked over and over to yield his hindquarters when he already knew how to do it? For us it would be like being asked to dig a ditch just so we could fill it back in. Just because we know how to operate a spade shovel doesn't mean that we're going to dig a hole in the backyard any time someone asks us to. There would have to be a dang good reason for us to want to expend that much energy. Why wouldn't it be the same for a horse?

After twenty minutes of showing me all the tasks the gelding seemed to have trouble with, the woman asked what I thought was the best way to get him to quit all his head shaking, tail wringing, and foot stomping. She seemed genuinely surprised when I told her I thought the best way to eliminate the problems was to simply stop asking him to perform the tasks.

"So," she asked, a bit confused, "I should just stop asking him to yield to pressure?"

"I didn't say that," I replied. "What I said was that I wouldn't keep asking him to yield to pressure *unnecessarily*. There's a difference."

"I see," she nodded. "So what should I do instead?"

"What do you mean?"

"What should I do to get rid of his attitude?"

I had to stop and think about that for a minute. You see, I thought I'd been pretty clear in my explanation that I felt the horse's attitude would go away when he was no longer asked to perform meaningless tasks. What I soon came to understand was that the woman was more than willing to stop using the techniques to get her horse to perform different tasks, providing I gave her a replacement technique to fix the problem. In other words, she couldn't see how her horse could learn something without her teaching it to him first. She figured before the gelding could lose his attitude, she needed to do *something* to teach him how to lose it.

"The only thing you need to do to get him to lose his attitude," I repeated, "is quit asking him to do things unnecessarily. Once you do that, the attitude will go away on its own."

She still seemed a little bewildered, so I went on to explain that sometimes, when we continually drill our horses on simple tasks that they already know how to perform, they become agitated with us. It's kind of like when we were in school. In first grade we learned that one plus one is two. Well, one plus one is still two in second, third, fourth, and every grade after that. Because we've already learned the answer to the question clear back in first grade, we are no longer drilled on it. We still use the premise of addition in our day-to-day activities, but we are seldom, if ever, asked that particular question once it's learned. If we were asked the question daily as we got older, eventually we would likely stand up and ask the teacher if we could move on to something else.

"I think it's the same in this situation," I told her. "He may just be telling you that he knows what one plus one is and that it's time to move on."

"Won't he forget how to yield to pressure though?" she asked.

"I expect he'll never forget that," I told her with a smile. "In fact, my guess would be that sometime you'll be grooming him or getting ready to saddle him, or something like that, and need him to move over for you. You'll touch his side, and he'll step right over without so much as a tail flick. The difference is that there will be a purpose behind the request instead of you asking him to move over, just to do it, like you are now."

"How would he know the difference?" she asked, with disbelief in her voice.

"I believe horses know the difference between when you are doing something *with* them and when you are doing something *to* them," I told her. "They're pretty sensitive animals and there's definitely a different feel between the two things that they pick up on, if you give them a chance. I expect that when you need him to do it for you, he will."

She thought about it for a little while and decided, because nothing else that she'd tried had worked, that it would at least be worth a try.

I mentioned that I thought her horse might also be getting a little frustrated and confused with the way she was leading him, as well. I pointed out that because she didn't have any set boundaries on what was an acceptable closeness between the two of them, he never knew when he was doing the right thing—the proper leading distance was a continually moving target for him. He might venture too close to her without even knowing it, and when that happened, she reprimanded him by shaking the rope at him. She had been setting him up to fail by not being consistent in her expectations.

Over the next several minutes, we worked on getting the two on the same page regarding an acceptable leading distance, which ended up being around three feet between them. As long as he stayed three feet or more away from her while they were walking, she just quietly went along her way. If he got any closer, I asked her to stop abruptly and, without shaking the rope at him, go over to him and ask him to step back to the three-foot distance by applying light, constant, backward pressure to the lead rope. Pretty quickly he had figured out the distance that she had in mind and, as soon as he did, he never once offered to breach it. Just like that, she no longer needed to shake the rope at him, and his head tossing and tail wringing went away.

More often than not, that's how easy it goes once our horses understand what we are asking of them. I don't know how many people I've seen who have relied so heavily on getting a certain technique just right that they have lost sight of everything else, including their horse. The sad thing is that it's usually those same people who are trying so hard to achieve a true, willing partnership between themselves and their horse. Unfortunately, the harder these folks strive for that kind of relationship relying strictly on techniques and cues, the worse the relationship often becomes.

Sometimes things deteriorate very quickly—almost overnight it seems—with the horse suddenly, and sometimes violently, protesting every little thing that the rider tries to do. More often than not, however, the relationship deteriorates at such a slow pace that the owner doesn't even realize anything is wrong until weeks, months, or even years after things originally began to fall apart. Even then, there is usually nothing that the owner can actually put a finger on. It's more of a nagging feeling that something just isn't right between them. Once the feeling starts, it usually doesn't take long before it gets the better of the person and they start looking for some answers.

Over the years Jo had found the lessons she'd taken to be fun and beneficial from a technical standpoint, but she was beginning to see that they could also be a little confusing and contradictory at times, particularly when she switched from one sport to another or from one trainer to another. Instead of things becoming clearer for her, it became harder for her to separate, in her own mind, what might be right for her and what might be wrong.

About that time, Jo took her horse to her first clinic. It was held near her home and was being performed by a well-known, "natural" horse trainer with whom she was familiar but had never seen in person. The clinic was an eye-opening experience for her and changed the way she was looking at and working with her horses. She became less interested in showing her horses and very interested in learning more about the horse as an animal and how to work with them using techniques that took what the horse was going through into consideration.

Back at home, she began experimenting with a number of the techniques she'd learned at the clinic and quickly got some very nice results. She not only used the techniques on her own horses, but also on a few others that she had been asked to work with, again with some nice results. Finally, she felt as if she was on the right path in her search for that piece of the puzzle she'd lost somewhere along the way.

As time went on, Jo decided that she would like very much to start a horse from scratch, using all the things she had learned along the way. The horse she found was a very nice, ten-month-old Appendix quarter horse named Treasure. Other than wanting to train the filly from scratch, Jo had no other specific goals in mind for her when she bought her. Her interest lay mainly in the progression of the young horse and seeing where it all might lead in the end.

Jo was in no rash with the filly, and so started her very slow and easy. She was more interested in doing things right than she was in breaking any kind of land-speed training records. She took her time as she taught the filly how to lead properly, to allow her feet to be handled, and to load into a trailer while she was a yearling. She also worked with the filly on allowing herself to be sacked out with tarps, blankets, bags, and the like, and did some other basic ground work, such as leading her over poles and showing her incidental things like jump standards.

Over the next two years, Jo and Treasure had progressed from light ground work to basic work in the round pen, to saddling and riding. By the time the filly was three, they were working on speed control in all three gaits, transitions, bending, turning, stopping, and backing. Everything had gone very well, but it was getting time to take the next step in the filly's training, and Jo wasn't exactly sure what that step should be. She decided to take Treasure to a clinic. The trainer she had gone to in the past had not changed his clinic format, and she felt they were already performing all the tasks that they would be asked to perform at his clinic if they went. As a result, she decided to take Treasure to another clinician with a similar training style.

Things went extremely well for both of them at that clinic, and Jo felt as though the two were beginning to form the kind of bond she had felt with the horses she had when she was very young.

When Treasure turned four, Jo became more specific in the things she was asking of her, and even then, things were still going along pretty well. However, there were times when Treasure became bothered by certain things, such as strange sights and sounds, and that worried Jo just a little. She figured that, with all the work she had done with Treasure, surely she should have been over most of the spooks.

This was one of the reasons that, by the time Treasure turned five, Jo was once again feeling a little lost. She began looking for someone who might be able to help her through the rough spots she was experiencing, and she began going to more clinics.

One of the philosophies she picked up at the clinics was that the horse had responsibilities during training and that the rider needed to make sure that those responsibilities were being met. The clinics were also pretty focused on achieving goals with the horses, and Jo was slowly, unwittingly, beginning to change her own focus from that of trying to understand the horse's perspective on things, to that of reaching the next rung on the ladder.

Treasure responded to Jo's new way of training with mixed emotions. At times she was extremely fluid and soft, at others she was bracey and uninterested in what was going on. There were times in the round pen when Treasure would look away from Jo, gazing over the fence during ground work. When that happened, Jo would put the mare to work by twirling her lead rope and sending her around the pen. In fact, sending the horse away from her was a big part of the training she had been practicing, and Jo was getting good at it. She would send her horse away while working in the round pen; she would send the horse away while backing her up. She would send the horse away to go forward. To move the hindquarters, she would send them away from her. It was the same with the front end. She would send the mare away to go out and circle around her, and if the mare didn't do it fast enough, she would send her away with more "life."

Based on what she'd learned at the clinics, Jo was sending Treasure away from her regularly, and the mare was beginning to understand that kind of behavior from Jo meant only one thing—that Jo didn't want the mare to be near her.

Over time, even though it seemed the mare *was* becoming more responsive, she also began to show signs of her disinterest and frustration at how she was being handled. This showed itself in a number of little ways that, in and of themselves, didn't mean much. But taken as a whole, they tell the story of how Treasure saw the situation.

Suddenly the mare, who was always interested in food, was the last horse out of the five Jo owned to come in out of the pasture at meal times. Jo noticed the sparkle that the mare usually had in her eyes was beginning to fade, and the mare seemed not to look forward to their time together anymore. In fact, Jo noticed that if she asked Treasure to stay with her in the pasture, round pen, or just about anywhere else, the mare would comply. But if Jo didn't ask, Treasure always left, turning her back and walking away.

Treasure's lack of enthusiasm was beginning to show under saddle, as well. Sometimes she would be soft and responsive to every cue that Jo gave her; other times the mare braced against the bit or didn't give to a leg cue, and Jo ultimately ended up increasing the pressure until she got the response she was looking for. Jo was doing what she had been taught at the clinics. She made the wrong thing difficult for Treasure. Unfortunately, because Treasure was such a sensitive horse, the mare began to worry about making mistakes, while trying to figure out a way to avoid the consequences that Jo provided. Even though, on the surface, Treasure appeared responsive most of the time, she couldn't relax. It was as if she was constantly in the "ready" mode, looking to react any time, anywhere. Unwittingly, Jo may have been making the wrong things *too* difficult for the mare, and as a result, the mare was building a wall between herself and Jo.

———————

It had been raining and cold since I first arrived that morning, and after having worked with six horses and riders, I was particularly thankful that we'd been in a covered arena all day. Even at that, I was going on my tenth hour in the arena, and the cold, damp weather was starting to get to me. All my past broken bones and old injuries were starting to flare up, and I could feel that familiar tightness between the left side of my neck and my shoulder blade that told me I was on my way to a painful muscle spasm before the day was over.

Some folks had toughed out the cold and were still in the bleachers, but the crowd had been dwindling for the last two hours. As i answered some questions from the spectators, the last horse of the day was turned loose in the round pen by her owner. The horse was a nice-looking quarter horse mare. As soon as the owner left the pen and closed the gate behind her, the mare took off for the other end of the pen and hung her head over the fence.

Just then it began to pour, and the sound of hay-bale-sized raindrops smacking the tin roof of the arena made it hard to hear what anyone was saying. Not only that, but it wasn't doing anything to help the already nervous horse standing in the pen. I made my way over to the round pen where the horse's owner was standing.

"It's Jo, right?" I asked, over the roar of the rain.

"Yes," she nodded.

"And your horse's name is?"

"Treasure."

"Okay, Jo," I said, as I moved a little closer so I wouldn't have to yell. "What did you want to work on today?"

"Well," she said, "to be honest, Treasure is a little farther along in her training than the rest of the horses that you worked with today." She paused, as the mare charged past us. "I guess I'd like to work on some flying lead changes."

"Okay," I nodded. "How's her ground work? Does she lead all right? Is she easy to catch?"

"She's fine with all of that," she replied. "In fact, we've spent quite a bit of time working on the round pen stuff, and she's pretty good at yielding to pressure. She's real easy to catch."

"She's a little nervous, eh?" I commented, as the mare made another lap past us.

"I haven't ridden her for a while, and she hasn't been off the home place in months."

"Okay," I nodded again. "Would you mind if I went in with her to see if we can get her to settle down a little?"

"No," she said. "Go right ahead."

With that, I went into the pen and moved to the center, where I watched the mare run circles around me. Now, I need to point out again here that the weather was unseasonably bad. It was cold and raining, and about the time I went into the pen, it began to hail. Even so, I was a little bewildered by the mare's behavior. There's no question that she was extremely upset by the weather and the noise from the roof as the rain and hail came crashing down, but I was surprised that she wasn't looking for some help. She remained on the rail and continued to make laps, even after I went to the middle of the pen and invited her to come in by me.

She made a lap, moving from a trot to a lope, then back to the trot, before switching directions on her own. Any time she even offered to glance in my direction, I would either step back or shift my weight backward in an attempt to draw her in, but she would have none of it. She was much too scattered, mentally. I decided I'd need to do something to focus her more on what was going on inside the pen, instead of what was going on outside. I stepped over to the rail as she came around and raised my hand at my side to about belt level in an attempt to get her to reverse directions.

What I saw next stunned me. The mare came to a very quick stop just in front of me and went through the quickest succession of responses I'd ever seen from a horse. In less than ten seconds, the mare fired off a yield on the forehand, a yield on the hindquarters, a back up, and a side pass. She then did a forehand move the other way, a side pass faster, moved her hindquarters the other way, side passed again, and did a few more things that I'd never seen, before coming to a complete stop and staring at me. I lowered my hand and stood in amazement at what I'd just witnessed.

"Dang," I heard myself say.

I raised my hand again, and the mare went through another rapid-fire succession of movements, each one meant as a question, asking me exactly what the heck raising my hand was supposed to mean. Of course, all I wanted was for her to reverse direction, but that was the one thing she didn't try. I lowered my hand and watched her as she stood staring at me.

It was obvious that a great deal of time, effort, and thought had gone into this horse's training, because she sure knew a great deal of "things." However, as I mentioned to Jo, one thing that bothered me was the way in which the mare searched for the answer to the question. There was no feel in what I had just seen; it was simply one mechanical response right after another. It looked to me as though the mare felt that she not only *had* to look for the answer but also felt she'd better, by God, get that answer right. I didn't get the impression that it was okay for her to simply stop, look at me, and say, *Hey, buddy, I have no idea what you want me to do.*

As far as she was concerned, it was completely unacceptable for her to communicate to me that she didn't understand what I wanted. It was not okay for her to give me her opinion. Instead, she said to me, *Okay, you're raising your hand and I don't know what that means, I'm not supposed to not know this, so here is every response I've ever been taught, and three or four things that I don't even know what they are—please tell me one of these is right!*

I'm going to stop right here and stress that I do not believe that this mare's responses had anything to do with her being physically abused in any way, shape, or form. That's what many folks might assume, and that simply was not the case. I felt I was seeing a horse on overload—too much information had been presented over the years, in ways the mare didn't always understand.

I worked with Treasure as quietly as I could for a little longer, and then asked Jo if she wouldn't mind getting saddled up so we could see how things were when she rode.

"You bet," was her response, even though there was a hint of defensiveness in her voice.

Jo came in and brought her saddle pad with her. She stopped a few feet from the gate and patted her hand on her leg. Treasure looked at her, dropped her head submissively, and started to walk toward her. That seemed a little odd to me. It was nice to see a horse be responsive to a command, but by the same token, it struck me that the mare was doing all the work. It appeared that she was expected to walk from one side of the pen to the other, without hesitation, so that she could stand and be saddled. Not an unreasonable request, I suppose. But it sure put an awful lot of pressure on the horse to do the right thing. After all, sixty feet is a long way to go without getting distracted or losing focus on the task at hand, particularly on a cold, rainy day like this. It seemed to me that there was a large margin for error on the horse's part. If she erred, what would the consequences be?

"What kind of relationship are you looking for with this horse?" I asked, as Treasure was halfway across the pen. Jo turned and looked at me.

"I'm looking for a partnership," she replied. As soon as she took her eyes off her horse, the mare stopped, turned, and began heading the other way.

Jo turned her attention back to her horse and patted her leg. The mare turned back around and continued toward her.

"If this is supposed to be a partnership," I asked, "then how come she's doing all the work?"

"What do you mean?" Jo asked, once again taking her attention off her horse. The mare hesitated, then turned and headed back the other way.

"Well, you want to put a saddle on her, right?"

"That's right," she said, as she patted her leg again.

"But before you can do that, you want her to walk all the way across the pen to you?"

"Is there something wrong with that?"

"Not really," I said. "It's just that it seems like a pretty one-sided partnership."

The mare was walking toward Jo, but this time Jo went over and met her halfway. She petted the mare on the neck, showed her the blanket, and slipped it nicely up on her back. Jo went to get her saddle from the top rail of the round pen, but as soon as she did, the mare turned and headed for the opposite end of the pen.

"What should I do about her walking off like that?" she asked, with a hint of frustration in her voice.

"I guess we could put a halter on her."

"But why shouldn't she just stand for me to saddle her? That's usually how I do it."

I told her it looked as though the mare was having some trouble standing still, what with the weather and all. So maybe, at least for that day, it wouldn't be so bad if we gave her a little help. With that, we haltered the mare. Soon she was saddled, and Jo was up and riding around the pen. Within minutes, she was asking the mare to perform some advanced moves, and the mare responded without hesitation. She did a turn on the forehand and side passed. From there she went forward, stopped, backed, brought her front end around, and then repeated the entire process, moving from one maneuver right into the next.

There's no question that Jo was getting the mare to do some nice things. However, each movement was accompanied by some kind of protest by the mare. A head shake here, a wringing tail there, pinned ears, or a general look of discontent followed nearly every step Treasure took. The mare was stiff through each maneuver and couldn't seem to follow through completely with any of them. In short, the mare was doing what she was asked, but she didn't seem to really like it much.

I was beginning to see that I might have a problem on my hands. Jo brought Treasure to the clinic in search of help, but I wasn't entirely sure that she would want to hear what I had to say after watching the two of them together.

"You mentioned that you're looking for a partnership," I said, as Jo pulled Treasure to a stop next to me.

"Yes," she nodded, as the mare fidgeted in place.

"What do you want your partnership to be based on?" I asked, as I reached over and stroked the mare between the eyes.

"What do you mean?"

"Do you want your partnership to be based on trust, mechanics, domination . . .?"

"Trust," she interrupted. "I want her to trust me."

That was the answer I was hoping to hear, but I still wasn't sure it would make what I was about to say any easier for Jo to take.

"Well," I hesitated. "I'm going to have to be honest with you here. I'm seeing an awful lot of mechanical responses from your mare without much feel behind them."

"What do you mean, 'mechanical'?" she asked.

I explained that it seemed as though her mare was responding not out of trust, but because she had been more or less "programmed" to respond. In other words, she had been drilled to the point that she felt that nothing short of perfection was acceptable. Because there was little room for error, Treasure focused on trying to get the task perfect, instead of putting her trust in and focus on Jo. By the same token, Jo's cues had become somewhat mechanical, as well. Just about everything she asked from her horse seemed to have a sort of "I say, you do" attitude behind it. It was entirely unintentional on Jo's part, but it was there nonetheless.

Because the mare was focused on the task and was responding to mechanical cues in mechanical ways, there didn't seem to be any way she could put her trust in Jo's judgment, particularly when it came to anything outside of the realm of the mechanics they had worked on. Since Treasure couldn't trust, she was never able to relax when people were around. She exuded the feeling of always being on edge, because she never knew when she was going to be asked to perform in one way or another. As a result, Treasure not only wasn't able to look for help from me that day, she was also having trouble with getting soft for Jo while under saddle.

I could see that Jo was upset with my explanation. Not wanting to make her feel any worse than she already did and seeing that more technique was not going to fix this problem, I asked them to do a couple of very simple maneuvers before suggesting that we quit for the day. I wanted to give Jo time to think about the situation, and I also wanted to give myself some time to think about what I could do to help them through it, providing Jo wanted to pursue it further when the clinic resumed the following day.

The skies had cleared somewhat by the next morning, but the air was still heavy and more rain was surely on the way. As I drove down the interstate on my way to the clinic, I wondered if I would see Jo there or if I'd upset her so much during our session the evening before that she had packed her things and headed for home.

I pulled into the arena and was happy to see Jo standing near the small corral that held Treasure. She noticed my truck and immediately headed over my way. I turned the ignition off and climbed out of the cab. Jo met me before I'd even gotten the door closed.

"I didn't get much sleep last night," she told me, with a sort of forced smile. "I laid awake thinking about everything we talked about yesterday, about how you felt Treasure didn't really trust me and how she seemed pretty mechanical." She paused. "I've had this mare since she was a long weanling. Everything about her, all the good and all the bad, comes from me. It's pretty fun to take the credit for the good, but not nearly as enjoyable to take the blame for the other."

I broke in and pointed out that I didn't want her to think there was anything wrong with how she'd trained her mare or even that there was anything wrong with the way the mare was responding to her. In fact, I told her that there was a whole lot more good going on between the two of them than there was bad. It was just that, in my opinion, if she was truly looking for a partnership with her horse, she may have been going at it in ways that made it more difficult for the horse to see it that way.

"I know," she nodded. "But I don't want her responding to me because she doesn't feel like she has a choice. I want her to do it because she wants to, not because she feels she has to."

"Fair enough."

"I guess I lost sight of how she felt about this whole deal," she began. "I was feeling pretty pleased with being able to push her through all of her various maneuvers. I never realized that she might have been detaching herself mentally from the whole thing. I don't want that for her, or me." She paused. "I'd like to do whatever it takes to make it right with her."

With that one sentence, I felt as though a huge load had been lifted off my shoulders. We began working on a game plan for the two of them for the next three days of the clinic. This plan consisted of little more than getting Jo to lighten up a bit, both physically *and* mentally. You see, Jo was a woman in a high-stress job geared toward achieving immediate results, from both her and her staff, on a daily basis. As a result, her motor ran pretty fast most of the time, even when she wasn't at work. Having a tightly wound spring may have been all right in her position as manager for a corporation, but Treasure never understood business management very well and so, more than likely, couldn't figure out why the two of them needed to be in such a hurry all the time.

I felt that was at the heart of the trouble they were having. Treasure was never given the time to think through the things that Jo asked from her. Jo had been taught during past clinics that if Treasure didn't respond within a given amount of time, pressure needed to be escalated until she did respond. That didn't leave much room for thought or error on the mare's part. It also didn't allow Jo the time she needed to *feel* the tries that Treasure offered. Jo often put a cue right on top of a try, which caused confusion for

Treasure. Treasure never really knew when she was doing the right thing and, as a result, had trouble being consistent in her responses. That, in and of itself, was one of the main reasons why the mare was soft and fluid one minute, then stiff and bracey the next. She simply never knew when she was doing something right.

Jo was a very quick study, and within minutes after beginning her session, she had already slowed herself down in the saddle and was softening the cues she gave. Treasure began the session almost as tense as she had the day before, but because Jo was waiting for responses instead of forcing them, the mare seemed to quiet herself down pretty quickly and her responses began to come with much more consistency. In fact, less than thirty minutes after starting, Treasure was performing all the things Jo had asked of her the day before, but she was doing them without the head shakes, tail wringing, bracing, or stiffness that we'd seen the previous day.

Over the next two days, Jo worked extremely hard on becoming even more consistent with her cues, as well as being consistent in the release of those cues. Treasure's responses became quicker and quicker, and her tries became bigger and bigger. Treasure's efforts thus became considerably more noticeable for Jo, who was then able to release her cues even faster, and often she didn't need to apply a complete cue at all. She just had to offer the cue, without actually applying it, and Treasure would respond correctly. Treasure's confidence and trust in Jo was growing right in front of our eyes.

By the fourth day, Jo had become so consistent and soft in the way she was cuing her horse that the mare would simply float from one task to the next without hesitation or protest. There was no longer the nervousness or feeling of her being on edge, and she seemed genuinely happy to be in the pen with Jo while they were working.

The change between the two of them was so dramatic that I was pretty sure they were over the hump as far as all the glitches in their relationship went. Jo was being quiet and consistent and had stopped trying to force the mare through things that she may have been having trouble understanding. She gave Treasure the benefit of the doubt more often and spent more time waiting for the mare to make the right decision in a tough situation, rather than trying to rush her. I felt confident that if Jo would just continue concentrating on these few things after she was back home, her relationship with the mare would continue to grow.

What I didn't know at the time was that all through the clinic, and even more so afterward, a cloud of discouragement had been hanging over Jo's head, Jo had been searching for years to find the "thing" that would be right for her and her horses. She was looking for that one technique or method that would bring the relationship together so that all would be well. What she was beginning to see instead was that technique and method had very little to do with building a relationship with her horse. There was much more to it, and now that she was beginning to see that, she felt that she'd let her mare down.

In the months that followed the clinic, Jo had an overwhelming feeling that she shouldn't ask anything from Treasure when they worked together. She felt tremendous guilt not only for putting Treasure through some of the things she had, but for the way she had put her through them. The guilt was eating her up, causing her to question every little thing that she did. She started to worry so much that she became almost paralyzed when they worked together. She found herself questioning her motives, sincerity, and goals.

Even though she didn't know it at the time, Jo had achieved what she had been looking for in her relationship with her horse.

Because Jo had proven her dependability, Treasure was beginning to look to her for support and guidance and was willing to follow her just about anywhere. However, when a horse is looking to you for direction and support, it probably isn't the best time to be carrying on a lengthy mental debate with yourself on how and what you should be doing next.

What Jo didn't know was that the mental vapor lock she was going through was happening because she wasn't looking to herself for the answers—she was still unwittingly relying on technique. The difference was that, instead of trying to see how fast she could accomplish a goal, as she had done before the clinic, she was wondering how soft was soft. But she didn't put any "feel" behind the question.

The voice on the phone was cheerful enough, but there was no question that something wasn't right.

"It's good to hear from you, Jo," I said. "How are things going?"

"Pretty good," came the halfhearted answer. "But I feel like I might be getting a little stuck again with Treasure."

Jo explained what was going on between the two of them, how she was questioning herself and her motives, and how she was afraid to ask anything of the mare. She was beginning to feel as though they were in a downward spiral, and she was concerned that they might not be able to get out of it. As I listened, even though Jo's concern was heartfelt, I couldn't convince myself that things were as bad as she thought they were. After all, the things that she was telling me had little to do with her horse or how her horse was acting. Most of what she was saying had to do with her inability to feel what was going on between the two of them. She was so concerned about what she should be doing and how she should be doing it, that she was missing the most important piece of the puzzle.

"I think what we need to remember here," I said, "is that your relationship with your horse comes from the heart, not the hands. From what you're telling me, Treasure is already there. She'll be waiting for you when you find it."

I made a point of telling her not to be so hard on herself, to try to quit worrying so much about accomplishing goals and doing "things," and to just enjoy her time with her horse. Once they were comfortable with each other, the goals and "things" would more than likely take care of themselves.

Months passed before I heard from Jo again. When I did, it was in the form of a letter. She wrote about some of the recent trail rides she and Treasure had taken. She began by telling me how she'd quit asking for "things" from the mare and was starting to simply spend time enjoying Treasure's company.

She mentioned that during one of the rides they took. Treasure was fidgety at the beginning, but by the end, she'd become real soft and quiet. During subsequent rides, the fidgeting went away completely, but as the rides went on Treasure sometimes became a little anxious. Instead of *making* her try to control her anxiousness, as she would have in the past, Jo allowed Treasure the opportunity to express her opinion. She allowed the mare to move when she felt like she had to, but Jo also stepped up and directed her in a soft and meaningful way, usually asking her to do some serpentines or figure eights around nearby trees and bushes. Jo mentioned that, even though Treasure was anxious, she remained soft in Jo's hands and never tried to leave, ran off, or quit. Each time, Treasure was able to calm herself down within just a few minutes and was even able to stop and stand quietly when Jo asked her to.

Jo told me in her letter how her relationship with Treasure was once again starting to blossom and, just within the last few weeks, they had had some of their best rides since they first began riding together some four years before. As I read the letter, I couldn't help but wonder if Jo had finally let go of relying on technique to help her through things. Then I came to the last few paragraphs of the letter and found the answer to my question.

"Things that I used to get from my horses, such as lead changes and four-stride trot/canter/trot transitions . . . I see those things now as gifts. Gifts that were in that moment, willingly given from my horse to me. I think there is definitely a connection between what I am able to give my horse and what the horse is able to give back to me.

"Things like technique, mechanics, and goals shouldn't ever compromise the gifts from the horse. If we begin trying to get those gifts 'on demand' or take the gifts from the horse, we can create some problems. You can ask for a gift, but you can't just take it. Taking too many of these gifts without giving enough back to the horse will run the risk of extinguishing the try in the horse and eroding the relationship between the horse and rider. So I'm thinking that these gifts simply have to follow a cycle. I give to the horse so the horse can give to me, and it just keeps going. And there is such joy in giving.

"Overall, I feel like I'm just trying to rediscover the connections I had with horses when I was just a kid and I rode by the seat of my pants and didn't 'know' anything. Not that there wasn't plenty of fumbling around on my part, but things always had a way of working out. The pure wonder and joy of just being on, or even around, horses. And of course that wonderful smell!

"I think I was riding with my heart and not my head back then. I was basing pretty much everything on feel because that's all I had. If I got too cocky, my horse would 'remind' me to pay attention to the

feel. Somehow I lost touch with that. Not totally, by any stretch, but I had lost some of it and I reckon that's what I'm trying to get back to.

"I have always had a habit of discounting my accomplishments or losing sight of them completely. Instead, I tend to put all the emphasis on the things yet to be learned or the 'problems.' That puts a lot of pressure on me *and* my horse. It is awfully easy to fall into the mode of nitpicking and nagging the horse, slipping into the 'problem-solving' mode—looking for the mistakes and then trying to fix them. I think that sometimes I may have unconsciously and unintentionally set my horses up (in small ways) to make some mistakes, so I could set out working on —fixing them. Testing the horse—to see where it was at and evaluate the holes that needed to be fixed. I know now I could have done a better job of acknowledging all the great things my horse and I were doing and spent less time focusing on what we weren't doing or what I thought we needed to do better.

"I'm not saying that I think goals are bad. They can give direction and purpose. But the problem I see with being too goal-oriented is that it can be awfully easy to lose sight of the moment, to become so focused on the destination that you miss the journey.

"I am beginning to realize that a person never gets 'there.' This is really a journey with *no* destination. It is an unending process. Everything that is important is 'as you go,' not 'when you get there,' because there is no there! It has taken me such a long, long time to realize this!"

And in those few paragraphs it became clear to me—Jo had found the key that unlocks the door.

Oftentimes we get so hung up on accomplishing goals or relying on techniques or methods that we don't allow that piece of ourselves—the piece that lets the horse know we can be trusted—to shine through. We can't force our horse to trust us. It doesn't work that way. Trust is something that must be earned. It has been my experience, however, that once that trust is earned, all the goals are so much easier to accomplish.

In the end, all we really have is ourselves and our horses. No technique, tool, or tack is going to change that. But then, I guess, when it gets down to it, perhaps it never should.

NOTES FOR THE CONNECTION

I remember wanting to use the story of Jo and Treasure in this final chapter to help illustrate not only how easy it is to get sidetracked from time to time with our horses, but also to show how easy it is to get back on track when we make the effort. What happened between Jo and her horse was certainly not an uncommon occurrence in the horse world, and I'm sure its something that has happened to all of us at one time or another.

Still, the point I hope that comes across here is how, by being able to take a step back and decide what is *truly* important to not only us, but also to our horse, that finding solutions that work for everybody can be found relatively easily. It is only when one or the other of us gets totally locked into our own opinion that problems can seem insurmountable. Something I like to try to keep in mind whether working with horses or people, or just getting through the day is that things are almost never as bad as they seem. They are, however, almost always as bad (or good) as we make them.